BREAK FREE

BREAK FREE

The Making Of An Entrepreneur

Robert F. McCusker

iUniverse, Inc.
New York Lincoln Shanghai

BREAK FREE
The Making Of An Entrepreneur

Copyright © 2005 by Robert F. McCusker

iUniverse books may be ordered through booksellers or by contacting:

iUniverse
2021 Pine Lake Road, Suite 100
Lincoln, NE 68512
www.iuniverse.com
1-800-Authors (1-800-288-4677)

ISBN: 0-595-34427-5

Printed in the United States of America

For
Agnes Marguerite Hurley McCusker
(1909–1993)

Straight Talk On Breaking Free From the Control of Others

This book discusses many of the subjective aspects of pursuing a livelihood as an entrepreneur. It avoids technical elements involved with operating a business. The reader envisioned as I reveal the essence of entrepreneurship in these pages was myself, twenty years ago, looking for road-tested concepts to guide our new agency business.

This practical book is written to help guide would-be and veteran entrepreneurs with solid basic ideas. And to help students and teachers with their teaching. It is not textbook, only an attempt to slip some wisdom into your brain food.

CONTENTS

FOREWORD

BREAK FREE is a window into the heart of a successful entrepreneur who measures success by the age-old standards of integrity, freedom, and valued relationships.

Bob McCusker understands the benefits of entrepreneurship in terms of personal freedom to create, and to serve clients and community. This book is about getting rich in ways more meaningful than money—through relationships and the building of social capital that is so vital to the fabric of a vibrant community.

Bob tells it all, from the positive thrill of a businessman launching out on his own—free from the demands of any boss or organization—to the negative thrill of starting over, with no money, as a shoe salesman. You can not learn the practical lessons of entrepreneurship any better than through real life experiences of one who put his entire net worth on the line to start his own firm. Bob's healthy balance of humility with self-confidence give him a wonderful personal platform. His message is one every aspiring entrepreneur should read before taking the big risk to go it alone in business.

~ Merrill J. Oster; Founder, Oster Communications, Inc.

Mr. Oster, an "Entrepreneur of the Century" in 2000, encountered Acres of Diamonds in his own back yard. Born Cedar Fall, IA in 1940; BA Iowa State, MS U. Wisconsin. 1969 founded Oster Communications and Farms, Pro Farmers of America; acquired Futures Magazine/FutureSource global financial news/analysis; founded Pinnacle Forum America; 2003 launched Iowa's largest planned real estate development in history; 2004 sold Oster Dow Jones and FutureSource, (part of OCI's 30-year sales =$1 billion.)

INTRODUCTION

Personal Freedom and Job Satisfaction Are
The Heart and Soul of Entrepreneurship

The secret to life?
Find something you love to do, then find someone to pay you to do it, or BREAK
FREE on your own.

IF YOU WANT to grow your own business, you can. Growing your own profitable business is a special sort of challenge. However, with the correct knowledge you can learn and understand how to profit, while free to "do what you love and love what you do."

This guide gives you elementary concepts, which I've refined from fifty years of business experience. Before riding off into the sunset, I want to teach you the concepts, or fundamentals, that are needed for guiding your business and enjoying your venture for a long time. They can strengthen your existing or new business: From the sweet flowers of self-renewal to the hasty weeds of self-employment taxes.

This slender volume can also improve your chances to quit your job, have more quality free time, and earn more money doing work you love by growing your own business, if that's what you desire. You'll find insights and enlightening stories to take you where you've never been before

This book is not for you if you're looking for quick fixes; it's about acorns to oaks,
not mushrooms.

It's about thinking long term, taking the time to get organized for The Jungle. It's about the secrets of self-confidence, self-renewal and job satisfaction.

SO, WHAT MAKES A BUSINESS PROFITABLE? Simply this: bringing in more money than you spend.

The early Internet companies focused on the more money part, then ignored the last three words. Major mistake. When their bubble burst the truth came out. The World Wide Web is not about making money, it's about *saving* money: Costs plunge, collaboration increases, productivity climbs and customer service soars.

Q: What do you need to make a success of your business? Location? Money? Ideas? When I quiz University business students with this question—as a visiting lecturer—the entire flock chirps cliché buzzwords, crammed into their bright minds: "Mission Statement ... Teamwork ... Human Resources ... Computer Systems ... Website ... Corporate Identity ... Image."

A: Customers. There are only a few of my true fundamentals underscored in this book. This is the mother principle of entrepreneurship:

1. *Identify Your Customers.* Without customers you cannot grow a business. Or, expand one. You must absolutely know who your customers are, will be, or where they'll come from. You should survey to learn how long it will take to get them creating your cash flow. No Cash, No Eat.

Here's how I learned this lesson the hard way:

LATE ONE SUNNY SUNDAY morning in January 1972, I flopped back onto the bed in the back bedroom of our rented one-and-a-half story house in Waterloo, Iowa.

I was exhausted, broke, the father of five—Tom, Annie, Mark, Dave, Patrick—youngsters lucky to have their loving mother staying at home to raise them.

I'd worked every day straight for 117 days, and I was due at a shoe store in our new mall to sell shoes part-time. Again. The same retailer had employed me thirty hours a week when I worked my way through college, along with my GI Bill monthly checks.

Fitting shoes on finicky female feet *again* had evaporated any remaining traces of excessive hubris from my crumpled ego; an indelible lesson in humility.

I stared at the ceiling, thinking of how I could face up to defeat, and tell my wife, Beverly, my business forms brokerage idea was a total flop. I'd sold our suburban four bedroom home overlooking Chattanooga, Tennessee and moved our family back to our hometown four months earlier.

Our modest equity cash was gone. My business forms sales didn't yield enough profit up front. Our car was worn out. I was worn out.

I felt like *Jack and the Beanstalk* after selling the family cow. I was a fool to have thought that long-term repeat business alone was the magic way to build a business of my own. There wasn't enough cash flow for current expenses.

I'd been making sales calls for McCusker Business Systems during the week, then selling shoes on the weekend. A humbling experience for a 36-year-old star salesman who had quintupled his income since his first year out of college, by managing a 3M Business Products dealership with a dozen employees.

Earlier, I'd traveled to many major U.S. markets training sales people how to sell Control-O-Fax bookkeeping systems for doctor's offices, which were produced in Waterloo.

What was I thinking? I can't believe what a stupid plan that was.

I believe I was convinced that 'hard work and a positive attitude' was the path to success. I had worked my derriere off.

Where was the success?

My ego wanted to be in business for myself, like some of my contemporaries in the office products field.

I was articulate, with twelve years experience, affable, and professionally attired in three-piece suits. But I must have been out of my state-college-educated mind; there was only a trickle of money coming into the house.

It was the 'Willy Loman' syndrome: I was just a salesman out there on a smile and shoeshine.

It was Vu Deja: Nothing like this had ever happened to me before.

How was I ever going to get us out of this hole?

CONSEQUENTLY, the next morning I'm sitting at my 'Mr. Big' executive desk jammed into Annie's back bedroom, which doubles as world headquarters for McCusker Business Systems, reading the Sales Help Wanted section from Sunday's *Des Moines Register*. One ad catches my eye: "New syndicated merchandising program for independent drug stores. Travel Iowa, salary, new car."

I think about that. Maybe I can get the salary and the new car, travel around the state for this outfit, *plus* sell my forms on the side at the same time; keeping my own business alive with a support system.

No, I don't want to be away from home anymore. I fling the newspaper into the wastebasket. Despair.

However, the rent is spent.

I've got to do something. I drag the newspaper out of the wastebasket and call the Detroit headquarters number:

"A-Mark Advertising, I'll connect you with our Midwest Sales Manager."

I make an appointment to interview in Des Moines the next day. Mr. Big Mike, a gregarious Arab American in a Jewish company, is the SalesBoss. He asks when can I pick up my new Chevrolet Impala and get started at $165 per week, plus commissions.

My heart leaps for joy. Grocery money!

Big Mike flies back into Des Moines again with appointments made in northwest Iowa. I pick him up, in my shiny new Chevy, and we get started on my training program.

The mass merchandisers are killing off the mom-and-pop corner drugstores all over the country.

A-Mark offers a complete package, turnkey deal: a printed direct mail shopper-mailer, and all the merchandise items inside. The hot sale items will pull in store traffic like these country pharmacists have never seen before; except over at the new K-Mart.

I watch Big Mike, following a canned spiel, presenting A-Mark's program to a druggist in Algona, while he fills prescriptions.

Over ten thousand dollars are involved. Finally, 'Dutch' the druggist agrees to test the deal once. We walk out with the order.

I don't believe what I'm seeing. For twelve years I've tried to convince buyers to spend a few hundred dollars on office products; they hate to spend the first *dime* on office products.

However, apparently most businesses have real money earmarked for advertising. BINGO!

Finally, I'm in the right business. McCusker Business Systems is history.

Over the next thirty years I'll be involved with every possible type of advertising and marketing: research, creative, and production; working with hundreds of clients, from Fortune 500 corporations to struggling non-profits.

I'll work for an art studio, a graphic design and printing center, an advertising agency, and finally grow our own agency—helping smaller-scale clients grow—in partnership with my wife.

YOU MAY BE WONDERING when I'm getting to the part where I tell you how to start making a ton of money; how to become a well-heeled entrepreneur in high-tech.

No, that's not what this book is about.

These concepts are about Breaking Free. Free to choose your vocation, your customers, your partners, your working place and hours; free to earn as much as you want, or only as much as you need to pursue your dreams. *You* decide.

You'll read how I chose to work: as Robert Frost wrote, "My object in living is to unite/my vocation and my avocation/as my two eyes make one sight."

Like the joys of cabinetmaking, less is more. Less worry for a more balanced life:

"My way was wise as you shall find,
it helps preserve your peace of mind."

HOW ARE YOU GOING TO BENEFIT from this book? We both know one-sided bargains don't last. What's in it for you?

If you allow me to engage your mind with the rest of my stories, you'll learn the other sound, true fundamentals. They are numbered, in boldface, plus some are also **_underscored_** for your review convenience: The BREAK FREE WAY, the heart and soul of entrepreneurship

I promise that all my examples, and principle guidelines are tried and proven in the jungle of day-to-day commerce. My topics and parables are about my business, but they apply to almost any business enterprise.

Indeed, whether you're an entrepreneur by desire looking to grow bigger with many employees, or by default hoping to quietly earn a living and maintain the status quo with a flexible lifestyle, these pages will give you some valuable ideas and a pleasurable read.

THIS BOOK IS A HYBRID of business counseling, inspiration, and real-life human-interest stories: Anecdotes, parables, lessons, a few verses and curious tidbits to get you thinking. It's meant for general business readers who appreciate good business acumen with a sense of humor.

Webster says that an anecdote is "a usually short narrative of an interesting, amusing, or biographical incident." D'Israeli said, "a good anecdote is often a mini-drama that helps us reflect on our own lives."

I've organized this book into eight chapters, more or less with the narrative in chronological order:

I, II, and III focus on concepts which arise when you consider growing a business for yourself, without all the usual jargon and get-rich-quick blather.

IV and V demonstrate how much of business success may depend upon being patient, while learning your trade better, to help reduce the odds of (gasp) failure.

VI, VII and VIII show you how to use some ideas we've employed to further the interests of our clients, since 1985.

YOU'LL DISCOVER WHY BREAKING FREE IS IN:
The Wall Street Journal opined on 11 October 2004, "It turns out this economic expansion is different from those in the past, but not in ways that many thought. New jobs are being created as usual, but they are different kinds of jobs. *The U. S. economy is undergoing a structural change as more people become self-employed or form partnerships, rather than working for large corporations.*" [Italics added]

LIMITATIONS: This book is mostly about marketing.
Not much here about finance, human resources, taxes, accounting, or other critical issues for your business.

However, nothing happens until somebody sells something. If I can help improve your chances of success by giving you just one or two good ideas, you'll have a fine investment and a good resource between these covers.

So, Dear Reader, come with me. As E.F. Schumacher says in the last line of his book, *A Guide for the Perplexed*, "It is desirable to leave these perplexities behind us and get down to work."

~ Robert F. McCusker

I: ELEMENTARY CONCEPTS FOR SUCCESS

Lessons For Your Business:
What the author learned from study, age and experience.

Robert McCusker at thirty-five in 1970 when he was V.P. & Gen. Mgr. of the Howell Co., a 3M Business Products Center in Chattanooga, TN. He had quintupled his income in ten years after college graduation, but yearned to 'break free and grow his own business.' He did. It flopped. [see Introduction]. That lesson of pain inspired him to seek the 'Mother Principle of Entrepreneurship.' He waited *fourteen years* to try it again in partnership with his wife, Beverly.

After high school, McCusker served two years non-combat active duty in the Marine Corps, in order to earn the G. I. Bill for his college education. Here, at the base camp of Mt. Fuji Japan, he had just came down from his mountain climb in 1955.

Two Wise Concepts From Exceptional
Twentieth Century Success & Achievement Thinkers,
Which You Can Apply to Your Own Life, Business

NIGHTINGALE'S SECRET: This is *the* one constant concept that has worked for the author for over forty years, detailed at length in this chapter. He heard Earl Nightingale speak at a high school graduation ceremony in Tipton, IA in 1959. McCusker's brother, William, had given a copy of this speech to him two years ealier. Both incidents left indelible marks on his business career.

Once one know's
Nightingale's 'Secret,'
the question remains: *Where* should one become a success? This handsome preacher, Dr. Russell Conwell, delivered his famous sermon over 6,000 times from 1888 to 1924:
'Acres of Diamonds'

2. Top Priority

IF I ASK what's your top priority in life, you'll probably list: religion, family, friends, favorite hobby; possibly you'll fib and list your job or profession last.

In growing your own business, your own fragile good health—*health capital*—is the ultimate factor. And remember, without your health you're no good to your family; they'll have to take care of you. That's a job they don't want.

Pay yourself first; exercise and eat well. You could be in for a tough year or two during a period of adjustment. Stay healthy. The good news: Leanness is nice ... but fitness is everything.

3. Feed Your Mind the Correct Knowledge

WITHOUT CORRECT NEW KNOWLEDGE you quickly become obsolete; without passion you wither. In either case, unless you're restless and growing, you're quietly going to seed. Make friends with your local library. It's free. Stay current.

I've always tried to remember this Chinese proverb: "Plan for a year, plant rice. Plan for ten years, plant trees. Plan for a lifetime, get more education."

4. Lacking Capital is No Excuse

WHETHER YOU just bought a new flatbed truck to make your mark with a construction company, or walked out on stock options at a FlopDot.com, lacking capital is no alibi.

You must avoid excuses if you expect to survive being self-employed. Consider *all* the various forms of capital:

Physical Capital—a truck or screwdriver—can increase production.

Human Capital—higher education or computer expertise—can enhance your knowledge and marketability.

Human capital accounts for 70% of the total capital in the USA due to our massive investment in public education.

Social Capital—refers to connections among individuals. If you invest the time and energy to network personally and professionally, when the moment of truth comes for you to build your own business, you'll be stunned as people come forward to help you get established. I was.

You'll have fear and doubt—as we all do—but you'll have more capital in your bank than you ever dreamed.

Research suggests the power of Social Capital; it can make you healthy, wealthy, and wise. Never underestimate the importance and power of your personal relationships.

5. Learn Your Terms of Persuasion

MR. JACK SHELLEY was a local boy from Boone, IA who made it in The Big Time. He was a World War II radio correspondent—Invasion of Europe, first A-bomb test, South Pacific with Marines, Japanese Surrender aboard the battleship Missouri in Tokyo Bay—then news director at Des Moines' WHO for many years.

He quit the media to teach Communications at Iowa State University, in Ames, IA, only a few miles from his birthplace.

I had the personal pleasure of working with Mr. Shelley when I recruited him at age seventy—after he retired from ISU—as the host and spokesman for a Boone bank's seniors club; one of my accounts at the agency I worked for in 1982. *He's 90-years old now.*

When he told his war stories to those Greatest Generation Americans, you could almost hear them all breathing. They'd been listening to him for forty years on statewide radio by then. What a great storyteller.

They tell me this is one of his teaching devices to help the college kids learn their business terms:

"When the circus is coming to town. A poster is placed in the window of the barbershop: that's *advertising*.

When the parade goes through town, a sign is placed on the side of an elephant: that's *sales promotion*.

When the elephant tramps through the mayor's flowerbed, but he issues a statement telling folks to attend the circus: that's *public relations.*"

6. Nightingale's 'Secret of Success'

MR. EARL NIGHTINGALE was a World War II ex-Marine, one of twelve survivors of the USS Arizona. He'd played Sky King in a 1950's radio serial, then toured as a motivational speaker.

After my Marine Corps duty tour in Japan, I had started college in 1956. My older brother Bill sent me a copy of a Nightingale speech in 1958: *The Secret of Success.*

Nightingale's speech to Maytag management had been copied onto Thermo-Fax paper. The first, but not the last time I was to see that brittle, buff stuff.

Nightingale remembered the discouraged faces of so many people during the Depression, when unemployment hit 25 percent. They blamed things and people; he knew because he asked them.

"Some blamed the Republicans, some blamed the Democrats. Some blamed Wall Street up in New York. Some blamed minority groups for taking all the jobs. They put the blame everywhere but where is it actually was: within themselves," Nightingale said.

Nightingale wanted to know what separated the Haves from Have-nots. It wasn't intelligence or I.Q.

It wasn't education.

He made up his mind about two things. At twelve years old, thirty-five seemed old to him, so he decided to retire at thirty-five.

Secondly, he decided to find the secret of success. It took him seventeen years to find it, then five years after that at age thirty-five, he did retire.

He thought surely someone else in all the billions of people must have figured this out, then wrote it down so others can find it in our wonderful free libraries.

All he could find was Albert Schweitzer's answer to a *Time* reporter's question about what was the matter with men today. "Men simply don't think," was his reply. "And eight out of ten who graduate high school will never open another book again as long as they live."

Next, Nightingale defined success as the progressive realization of a worthwhile ideal. i.e. a person knows where he is going, and is on the road to get there.

He said, "Virtually all women are successful and 98 percent of men fail. Because women want to get married to a nice guy and raise a family. That is their ambition in life, and they achieve it; maybe that's why they live longer?" (Not sexist in those times).

He proceeded to add a parable of a ship reaching its port because the crew followed charts and plans.

Finally, his distilled secret:

7. *"You become what you think about."*

"Here is an incredible law of cause and effect which completely removes fear and doubt as to whether or not we can achieve our goals. Everything you really wanted with all your heart you have gotten. And you are today exactly where you want to be."

This same fantastic law that will get you that new car you wanted, or helps you write a book like the one before your eyes, can be put to use for other objectives.

The chance to quit your job? You could lose your job in a thousand ways. There is no security. Do you want opportunity? More free time? Independence?

Why think about what you want to become, then listen to your heart? Even songbirds need Freedom.

A caged Nightingale loses the will to sing.

SUMMING UP: A wise man once put it this way. Your thoughts become words; your words become deeds; your deeds become habit; and your habits become your destiny.

So, you may want to consider one of my poems below; it's been my North Star for many years:

LOVING WORK

Was this the star to help guide you,
if someone asks, "What do you do?"

Perhaps your work is less in pay,
so grateful be if you can say:

"I love my work, I never miss,
I have a job that gives me bliss."

Why try to be the highest star?
Be happy you are who you are.

Be glad today you are alive,
not working merely to survive.

My way was wise, as you shall find,
it helps preserve your peace of mind.

8. Where to Find 'Acres of Diamonds'

MY WIFE AND PARTNER, Beverly, showed the lady with two younger children into my office, on the second floor of our 1910 two-story duplex; our residence was on the first floor in those days.

In 1990, our agency was in its fifth year of profitable operation. A satisfied client had referred the lady to us.

I always move out from behind my desk—a nearly 100-year-old family table—to make visitors comfortable. We all sat down.

Ms. Porter was a small person. Her clothes were quite plain, her hands were rough, red and chapped. Her children were well behaved and courteous. She told her story, which I'll always remember:

Her husband was unexpectedly out of work in a nearby, small rural Iowa town. They had no money, minimum education, and a family to feed. What did she do?

She didn't blame the rotten farm economy, political parties, lack of education, small-town isolation, or lack of funds for women's minority-owned businesses; she didn't seek welfare or faith-based charity.

She didn't view herself as a *victim*.

Little Ms. Porter looked out across the rolling hills of Iowa cornfields, and saw a valuable, free raw material: corn husks; the dry, brittle leaves covering the mature golden ears protecting Iowa's cash crop: 50,000 square miles of corn-husks—just waiting to be made into handcrafted dolls.

She had her own two hands, plus the hands of everyone else in the family.

She created exquisite 8–12 inch female dolls with long flowing dresses, complete with big frilly bows around the hems; huge floppy hats covering tresses almost reaching the ground.

Baskets of flowers were tucked under their tiny arms; areas of the natural beige husks were dyed to create different colored dresses. They were drop-dead adorable.

To each doll she attached a parchment paper label: Porter Originals ... an Iowa Product by Jane Porter; inside, a brief legend about the American Indian craft of husk doll making.

Pure wholesome gifts, welcome on every little girl's toy shelf, or as a decorative item for big girls.

Ms. Porter was selling the dolls through gift shops. She wanted to advertise in the trade journals read by shop owners. We provided a list of publications for her to contact with news releases, then test small ads in the Marketplace/Classified sections.

I told her we were flattered, and honored to be of assistance; she didn't owe us anything at that time for our brief conference.

In my office today, three faceless Jane Porter Originals are guarding over me as this is written; silent testimony to the 'Acres of Diamonds' in our own backyards.

Footnote: 'Acres of Diamonds' was a famous sermon by preacher and educator Dr. Russell Conwell, delivered over 6,000 times from 1888 to 1924.

9. Your Credit Rating

YOUR CREDIT RATING is the goose that lays the golden eggs. Regardless of how low your cash gets or what circumstances befall you—through misfortune or your own errors like me—you must preserve your reputation for meeting your obligations.

At our lowest point, after the whimpering end of McCusker Business Systems, before my advertising career paid off, we resorted to a household goods small loan. Instant credit card loans weren't available yet.

For weeks after, I wondered if Vito-the-Kneecapper would knock on our door to put mortgage tags on all our living room furniture, which we'd purchased during flush times in Atlanta.

We've never missed a due date since.

10. Embrace Change; Then Kiss it on the Lips

MY FRIEND, Dr. Bill Greer, was Dean of the College of Business Administration at my alma mater, now named the University of Northern Iowa. I serve on the advisory board for the Dept. of Marketing.

We also worked together on a public relations program for one of our clients: the MATT PARROTT Integrity Awards. More about that in chapter VI.

Once, we were discussing the lengthy process of revising the college curriculum; it takes about two years to get something changed.

"How many college professors does it take to change a light bulb," Bill asked.

"I give up," says I.

"CHANGE???!!!!" Dr. Bill said.

11. On Hiring Salespeople

WHEN HIRING SALESPEOPLE there are three key characteristics to look for. You can train them on all the other elements of your business.

Just be sure they have: Energy, Honesty, and Enthusiasm. [More on this later in the book.]

12. On Taking in Partners

KINKO'S was founded by a college student, Mr. Paul Orfalea. He just happened to have kinky red hair; naturally his childhood buddies nicknamed him Kinko. He knew that was a memorable name, so he applied the name to his business; the rest—as they say—is history.

Kinko's started growing into a national chain—now over 800 locations—by franchising with a twist. Each local investor also owned a piece of corporate head-quarters. i.e. they're all in it together.

But Kinko's gave it one more twist. You had to work with them for three years before you could buy in. He figured it takes three years to really get to know someone; you can fake it short time.

So, if you're considering a partner for business, or matrimony, be sure you've known him or her at least three years. It's absolutely the best if you can have your partners from Day One in business. You'll share all the triumphs, and heartbreak memories together.

Harmony is more important than a few bucks.

13. Where Profit Comes From

MR. WALTER V. GRAVES of Atlanta, GA was an ex-Marine, managing a Goodyear Tire store when I met and recruited him as a field sales rep in 1966. He shared the eight-states Southeast area with me when we were selling the Control-O-Fax bookkeeping system for doctor's offices.

Walt went on to found several enterprises of his own, all very profitable. We are still dear friends to this day.

When I first interviewed Walter for the sales rep job, I claimed it was quite interesting work.

"Bob," he drawled with that sweet, soft Georgia accent that Beverly loves, "I found Boys Scouts to be interesting. But I found Girl Scouts to be *rewarding* ... so, I prefer rewarding work."

And that's why he got the job.

Your business must be rewarding, as well as being interesting: it's called selling at a profit.

One banker asked, "If wages come from labor, and rent comes from real estate, and interest comes from savings, where does profit come from?"

"Answer ... Risk."

14. Measuring Your Prospects

YES, WE DO NEED new customers and clients. They're the lifeblood of your business. But, not just any customers. You need a yardstick to measure their worth to your operation. Here's how we measure potential clients:

1) Can you get the immediate order?
2) Will you have a satisfied customer?
3) Will it be a long–term relationship?
4) Is there repeat business?
5) Can you get strong referrals?

15. Incorporate? Avoid Needless Paperwork

SHOULD YOU INCORPORATE? Almost everyone you meet, and every book you read when you start your own business says you should.

We never did get around to it. We keep the books as a single proprietorship. Keep it simple. The simple life sets you free. Resist busy work paperwork.

Those legal men lawyers and accountants created the bogeyman *personal liability,* which should give you pause. However if you show suppliers and creditors that your name on the dotted line means your tail is also on the line, there are some intangible benefits of credibility, and respect plus the simplicity.

If you're not comfortable putting your tail on the line ... then maybe the little voice in your head is telling you to back off and pass on some particular deal.

Full disclosure: I'm not an expert in this arena. But why do things blindly because everyone says you should? Being an entrepreneur is partly about being intensely independent.

Furthermore, why should Mom-and-Pop work non-stop on paperwork, the barnacles of business?

II: ELEMENTARY MARKETNG

'Just go out and beat the bushes,' they said.

['How to fail as an entrepreneur.']

The author as model in 1978. He took part in a Meredith Corp test-marketing cover program. Focus groups of women, with electronically-wired reaction data, revealed that he should keep his day job.

By Groundhog Day in the nation's Bicentennial year, 1976, McCusker had developed his sales strategy and techniques to secure a 'Taj Mahal' of all sales brochures project for Winnebago Motor Home Industries in Forrest City, IA. While out on a highway, he experienced one of those rare 'Road to Damascus' moments that shaped his career for the rest of his life.

16. The Twin Battering Rams of New Business

LET'S REWIND TO 1972, when the Mr. Big Mike from A-Mark advertising in Detroit turned me loose on my own. Developing new accounts all over Iowa's ninety-nine counties was my challenge.

How do you do that?

After signing up 'Dutch' in Algona, we picked up a few more first-timers in northwest Iowa: Sheldon, Le Mars, Hawarden and Sioux City.

A-Mark used an effective tactic of working through the drug wholesale houses; their well-entrenched salespeople invited the druggists into an evening dinner-sales-pitch.

The gospel-tent effect helped the druggists confess their sins of complacency and face the damnation of going to hell-in-a-handbag-extinction by mass-merchandisers.

Traditional druggists came forward to be saved by our six-time per year, seasonal merchandising package: e.g. garden hose, plastic clothes baskets, food items.

"HALLELUIAH! SIGN HERE, PRESS HARD, THERE'S THREE COPIES. GREAT THINGS ARE GOING TO HAPPEN IN YOUR STORES."

Well, I can report from experience that clients have a way of waking up from these dreams of greatness. At some point the Power of a Plan has to take over.

That's where the Account Executive or Copy-Contact person has to deliver the goods.

I began to baby-sit those first trial accounts to the point where I knew what grades their kids were getting at school.

I made sure all their goods were properly delivered, then displayed; all the price tags were applied to create visual excitement at the Point-Of-Purchase. I focused all of my time, and attention to that northwest corner of Iowa; those few new accounts saw a lot of me.

Big Mike suggested I start working all over the state. I ignored him.

After the sales circulars hit the mailboxes, the folks poured in to swoop up the bargains. Success. All of my first-timers signed on again to keep the program rolling through the six psychological selling seasons: Holiday, Mid-Winter, Spring, Summer, Back-to-School, and Harvest.

My strategy of *Concentration* continued for eighteen months. I had the highest retention rate in the USA for A-Mark. Referrals kept coming.

By then I had traveled all ninety-nine counties of Iowa. We had an outstanding business going, after starting from scratch. Some of those first-time accounts are *still* using this type of program today.

When I tell this Concentration story to University students, I use the true story of the battle at the Golan Heights during the Arab-Israeli War of 1967.

The Syrians held deeply bunkered defensive positions, on a wide front over-looking the Jordan River valley. On June 9–10, under cover from the Israeli Air Force, the engineer troops built access roads up the steep slopes, then followed with repeated frontal assaults by tanks and infantry.

By concentrating their firepower so acutely, as a spear point, the Israelis pierced the line but not without great cost of casualties. The Syrian defenders fled.

The war was over in six days, saving many lives, which would have been lost if it had dragged on longer.

Victory, or success, isn't cheap; but it doesn't have to be needlessly expensive either.

SO, HAVE YOU figured out what's the other twin battering ram for new business? Did you note when I described the battle of the Golan Heights, I reported the Israelis made '*repeated* frontal assaults'?

Repetition is the twin of *Concentration*.

They are the battering rams for new business. Over the next thirty years I would prove this fundamental truth to myself, time and time again, beyond any doubt:

17. Concentration X Repetition = Effectiveness

Note, that's *times*, not plus. The repetitions are multipliers; stronger relationships make the sales effort easier, which means lower costs for your company.

In more comprehensive, advanced marketing books these strategies and techniques may be called 'Reach and Frequency.'

18. You Better Be running

EVERY MORNING in Africa, a gazelle wakes up.

It must outrun the fastest lion or it will be eaten. Every morning in Africa, a lion wakes up. It must outrun the slowest gazelle or it will starve to death.

It doesn't matter whether you're a gazelle or a lion.

When the sun comes up ... you'd better be running.

~ Anonymous

19. Finding Your Niche

YOU KNOW you can't be all things, to all buyers.

But, you can be all things to a few buyers. It's called segmenting the market. Here are a few of the demographic factors to help you decide your concentration strategy—i.e. finding your niche.

- ~ Geographical area
- ~ Type of prospect
- ~ Age groups
- ~ Income levels
- ~ Heavy users
- ~ Centers of Influence

You should focus on what you have, rather than worrying about what you don't have. If your soap product contains a lot of grit, better target the guys with dirty hands, not the ladies with delicate skin.

If your target audience is bored with 'Prunes,' start calling them 'Dried Plums.' Prove once again, that you *can* fool some of the people all of the time. (That's a joke).

Research suggests most buyers want the same things, in this order of importance: 1) Everyday low prices, 2) Wide selection, 3) Convenience.

RECAP: Who is your target audience? What benefits do they want? What does the competition offer them? If you know the answers to those key questions, you're on the right path.

Staying on the right path is easy. But, people like to get distracted, then wander off in different directions. The maxim of 'Shoemaker stick to your last,' is an old-fashioned way of finding your niche in business.

Then you should apply one-step-ahead concepts of continuous improvement, or you'll be lion lunch.

20. Experience Does Pay

GOOD JUDGMENT comes from experience; but some experience comes from bad judgment. Oops.

Sometimes, when we get a new client with a sense of humor—I hope—I tell them, "Right now you have the money, and we have the experience. In six months, we'll have the money and you'll have the experience."

21. Do You Really Understand Capitalism?

JUNIOR ACHIEVEMENT classes are a challenge: how should you explain economics to eighth graders? Here's how I once handled it for a class I visited as a volunteer:

"What's the difference between Capitalism and Communism? Let me explain it this way:

Suppose I give you all a test with a passing score of 75 percent. Some of you will achieve 95 percent, most of you will get 75, but a few will get 55 percent.

So, most of you will pass, but a few will fail; perhaps be held back until you learn how to bring your performance up to the mark ... or learn to like milking the cows twice a day for the rest of your lives.

Under Communism, 20 percent will be taken from those with 95 and given to those with 55; now everyone has 75 percent. Right? Raise your hands if you think that's a good system."

Lots of hands shot up.

"Now let's see the hands of those who believe all of you would continue to strive to get 95 percent."

No hands.

"And that, my young friends, is the difference between Capitalism and Communism."

On 31 December 1991, the Hammer & Sickle came down in Red Square; they locked the doors, and threw away the keys to the USSR. Go USA.

22. On Working With Successful People

BEING AROUND SUCCESSFUL PEOPLE will rub off on you. Quite the opposite effect of what your mother told you about hanging out with those bums down at the pool hall, or arcade, after school.

Harvey Penick, the legendary golf teacher, told Tom Kite, U. S. Open winner, to go to dinner with the good putters. Well, I don't know about that, it never worked for me.

During the mid 1970's I worked for a Waterloo-based art studio. One of my key accounts in Des Moines was the century-old publisher of famous titles.

I learned a lot from the staff at *Better Homes & Gardens (BH&G)* magazine, where I started my way through the Meredith maze of cubicles each week: cover design, the art and science of blurbs on the covers for retail point-of-sale, and the importance of consistency with reader expectations.

For example, the July issue of BH&G had better have a cover photo of strawberry shortcake on it, or heads would roll. If the art director had bought into Bob Furnsteneau's over-the-top idea, it would have sounded like Saturday night in the bowling alley. Bob was always pushing the envelope in cover design.

About this time, Meredith was going high-tech by measuring reader reaction to covers; a hocus-pocus focus group of ladies were wired up with sensors to record emotional response to potential cover concepts.

My amusing pal Bobby thought that those 7 million women readers would respond to a cover concept of "HE COOKS", with a photo of a middle-aged Everyman in the kitchen. "McCusker" he grinned, "you're my model."

Wow. So many women ... so little time.

SO WE HAUL a bunch of props out to Jim Autry's home for a high-class location, along with a food stylist and a crack photographer. We shoot away all afternoon. I'm looking good in a turtleneck sweater and pin stripe apron, of all things. Dreams of fame creep into the ego.

Bob puts together the mock-up cover, along with seven other traditional covers: strawberries, flowers, room settings, blankets, needlework and so forth.

The covers are shipped to California for the research outfit with the all wired-up women. The jury is out.

Weeks later, as I enter Bob's cubbyhole, he hands me my mock-up cover, which was tested.

"Your rating among the eight covers is noted as the number on the back side, in the upper right corner," he said.

I flip it over ... NUMBER EIGHT.

"Well, we learned something; strawberry shortcake is tough to beat, so your photo story will stay inside the book, toward the back," Bob said. "Better keep your day job."

23. Beware of Shoestring Accounting

WHY IS IT someone is always doing a seminar, a book or a trade journal article titled 'Marketing on a Shoestring.'

John Graham, in *NATIONAL CLOTHESLINE*, a monthly publication for drycleaners makes that point succinctly. He asked why doesn't someone write about "Accounting on a shoestring?"

Or, 'Manufacturing on a shoestring?'

Graham said, and I concur, marketing on a shoestring is a myth. Marketing costs money.

Building your brand takes a series of investments: some large, some small, some short term, some long term, but never ending.

And I say, that like the children who have eaten their cake and those who still have theirs, accountants and advertising agents are natural enemies.

So for a change, let's just see how the accountants like the shoestring treatment.

24. Ban the U-Word

IF I EVER stoop to the most over-used word in advertising—*unique*—right then, Beverly has instructions to throw the switch to the wires connected to my chair. I'm toast.

She has my epitaph picked out:

Here lies my Bob,
Here he does lie;
Now he's at rest,
And so am I.

25. How to Play Customer Golf

SHOULD YOU LET THEM WIN? No. *Never.*
The trickier question is, should you let them get away with cheating?

Playing golf with customers is not about getting their business. It's about *bonding* with them after you have their business.

A high percentage of your customers do enjoy the game, so it's a great way to spend four to five hours and really get to know them.

Each spring, after the art studio business was well established, I hosted the Meredith art buyers to a golf outing. The entire event cost the studio less than a big dinner and night on the town. No hangovers either.

For more intimate outings, I keep it to a foursome.

The BH&G guys bet me I couldn't break 90 strokes on one of their local municipal courses the first time I played it.

Waveland Golf Course takes a beating from the hackers, so when they held me to the absolute rules of golf, which do not allow nudging the ball to improve the lie, I knew I was in trouble from this humbling game.

Sure enough, on the last hole, my drive came to rest in a Grand Canyon of a divot. I barely advanced the ball. A bogie five gave me a 90. I lost a few bucks to each of them. They loved it. But, I lost fair and square.

THE NEXT TIME, we go to Jester Park, a wonderful county operated course. This time we play partners. Bob Furstenau, my graphic designer pal, and I take on the magazine's top art director and his associate director for a few bucks.

We're all square after thirteen holes. On the fourteenth hole, a par three across a pond, the art director splashes his tee shot into the water. He tees up a second ball, hits it onto the green and two putts.

As we walk toward the next tee he says he had a three.

"You had a five," says I, "two tee shots, a penalty and two putts."

"That first ball was a practice ball. I had a *three*," says he.

Right here, I should tell you that I'm seven-eighths Irish, and he has a Cockney accent.

"You had a *five*" says I.

After my remark, you cannot believe how l-o-n-g the rest of the afternoon was, or how frigid it can be at mid-summer in Iowa. Or how chilly it was near the art director's office for the next few weeks. I was lucky he didn't figure a way to ban me from the Meredith headquarters for good.

Was it worth it? No.

Is there a better philosophy to handle those situations?

Yes. It's called Yield and Overcome.

26. 'The Old is Forever New'

CONCENTRATION AND REPETITION worked yet again with Mutual of Omaha. My tortoise-like trips around the circuit of prospective accounts yielded a juicy illustration project for Gary Kelley.

After we gained the confidence of George Georgeff, the gentlemanly art director, with smaller projects, he commissioned the art studio to create Mutual's popular 'Wild Kingdom' calendar for their thousands of agents. Mutual's television series, by the same name, paved the way for that calendar.

The Bicentennial—1776–1976—provided the theme for featuring North American animals: beaver, buffalo, prairie dogs and others. Kelley did thirteen exquisite ink and water color paintings for that keepsake year. I saved a copy in my 'swipe-files.'

Twenty-five years later we used the same style layout for our millenium calendar project: 'Cedar Valley Entrepreneurs of the Century: 1900/2000.'

The 3M Company's old sales training program was titled 'The Old is Forever New.'

Always remember: 'Plagiarize, plagiarize/Never forget what goes/Before your eyes.' ~ Anonymous *(Naughty!)*

27. Ignore Intimidation: Groundhog Day I

ON GROUNDHOG DAY in our nation's Bicentennial year, I drove 115 miles from Waterloo to Forrest City, IA, pop. 4,200, the county seat for Winnebago County, on the Winnebago River.

Yes, it's the headquarters for the 2.4 million square foot Winnebago Industries manufacturing center.

Founded in 1958 by John Hanson, Winnebago's flying 'W' logo was king of the road in the Recreational Vehicle motor home category. Oddly, their success was related to a devastating fire, which reduced their first plant to cinders. When they rebuilt in 1966, their humongous space was devoted to motor home assembly on a massive basis.

My usual contact, Loren Swenson, the printing and graphics supervisor, had arranged a meeting for me with the person responsible for marketing services in their new product division.

I had a firm 9:30 a.m. appointment, so I left home in the dark for the long drive through snow-covered cornfields. I drove two and one half-hours to get there at the rigidly enforced 55-MPH speed limit, caused by the OPEC oil crisis.

AT 9:30 SHARP I PRESENT MYSELF to the Receptionist and ask to see my man. She calls his office to be told he'd left to attend an urgent ad agency meeting in the Twin Cities. Could I come back another time?

"Sure." I start driving back down highway U.S. 69 into the glare of the low southeast winter sunshine.

In my heart, I was disappointed that all my preparation of this seedbed wasn't to bear fruit quite yet.

In my gut, I was slowly realizing how I allowed myself to be intimidated by the image of this middle-of-no-place Fortune 500 wagon maker.

In reality, I had information and services they needed badly.

"Robert" I say to myself, "pull over and figure this out."

I tell myself it's time to show some guts with this Big Boy. Why should I accept being brushed off after investing the effort to get to a meeting they arranged?

Why can't I ignore that power; all those suits, those legal departments, and accountants? Why let them get away with this?

I'm 40 years old, my advertising apprenticeship is about over; I'm almost a 'Marketer' now, so I'm not going to take this crap anymore.

Like Saul on the road to Damascus, I pull a U-turn, then march back up to that sweet Receptionist, and tell her I'm there to "get started on a special project" for their new division. Could she do some further checking?

She calls the president (gasp) of the new division and asks if he knows anything about my special meeting.

"Yes sir, I'll send Mr. McCusker right over" she said. She directs me to the president's office a few blocks way.

"Now we're talking Bobby Boy," I say to myself. *Those five minutes out on U.S. 69 turn out to be absolutely pivotal in my career.*

The new 'LIVING COMPONENTS Division' of Winnebago Industries was a diversification effort spurred by the energy crisis of 1973 when gasoline prices quadrupled overnight. Their sales of behemoth motor homes went straight south; red ink flowed as engineers struggled to boost mileage.

Winnebago was re-directing part of their expertise for building prefabricated structures and rooms into the modular construction of family dwellings, motel and nursing home units. It was an enormous commitment of corporate assets and millions of dollars were gambled.

And I'd just bluffed my way into the game.

While I waited, briefly, in the division CEO's outer office, I chat up two foreign visitors.

First, there's a rumpled Russian who claims he'd gotten cosmetics giant Revlon into the USSR for a commission of $18 million. He's there to see about buying 4,000 room units for the 1980 Olympics.

Also, I meet a turbaned man from Saudi Arabia who wants 3,000 units for housing in the Middle East.

"Cash? No problem. My oil business is fabulous."

I'm hoping I still have my emergency C-note in my wallet to take the CEO to lunch.

The CEO takes me completely into his confidence. He introduces me to his top team of engineers and production people, also the son of the founder who's currently running the entire corporation, and finally 'Himself,' elder John Hanson, who happened to walk by.

Then we tour the production facility for several hours, have a *free* lunch with more teammates. The CEO explains how important the introductory sales literature is for the success of their marketing.

However, he's impressed by our wide experience with the BH&G floor plans, isometric and perspective illustrations, the general excellence and flair of our portfolio, and he expects great things from us.

Not to worry. We shake hands, then I'm out the door and on the road again; my memorable day ends as I slip into Waterloo-Cedar Falls at sunset.

The next morning I call the fellow who stood me up the day before to attend his Twin Cities meeting. I detail for him exactly what I did—without anyone's permission or purchase order—then hold my breath.

Long pause. "Well, you're just what I'm looking for; someone to bite the bull on the horns and see it through with their own initiative," he said. "Keep me posted, just keep working directly with the new division. Thanks." Click. I started breathing again.

THAT PROJECT TURNED OUT to be the biggest single brochure project in the history of the art studio; middle five figures with the printing included. Many other projects followed as I eased my way into other departments over the next year.
Don't let the size of the buyer, or deal, intimidate you.

28. Invest in Yourself: Groundhog Day II

ON GROUNDHOG DAY exactly one year later, I was the featured speaker for the monthly meeting of the Des Moines Advertising Federation. Around 100 members attended.

It was an ideal setting to promote the art studio, and network professionally with clients, prospects, plus adding to my personal 'Social Capital' account.

My Toastmasters Club training always helps me.

An obvious story to share that day was about my adventures 365 days before at Winnebago. So, I detailed my LIVING COMPONENTS brochure project—leaving out the U-turn epiphany—telling about the excited engineers, marketing service folks, and the foreign visitors from Russia and Saudi Arabia. Red-meat stuff for this audience, I thought.

"Now for the real kicker," I said, "in December 1976 the announcement was made—after an eighteen minute Board of Directors meeting—that Winnebago was quitting that type of business. Merry Christmas.

"The division was closed. The labor force went back into the RV production; my marketing contact guys scattered across the country. One of them said, 'You sleep with big dogs, you get big fleas.'

"Apparently, the USA had gotten used to higher gasoline prices. And elder John Hanson had pulled the rabbit out of the hat again with better mileage units: 'We're on the road again' was back in style."

I went on to mention other high-profile bankruptcies and failures: Penn Central R.R. and W.T. Grant, which had succumbed to discount mass merchandisers.

"Why tell these downer stories to this audience?

Because no matter how solid a business may be, or how big today, tomorrow is another matter. Your customer/client list can change drastically due to all sorts of events: mergers, takeovers, adverse court rulings, unexpected competition, even the local newspaper editor's favorite subjects—wars, weddings and weather—all forces beyond your control.

"The moral? Not every story has a happy ending. You need to face Reality.

Your best defense is to _invest in yourself:_ Higher education, evening classes, professional clubs like this one, Toastmasters Club, your own private course of study in areas of weakness, practice new skills, invest in new technologies, get in shape physically.

"Our fabulous libraries are free. Feed your mind ... Read ... Learn ... so you'll have the greatest trading power.

In the future, if you ever need to grow your own business, it's doubtful all of your customers will quit you on the same day.

"If you get started with these personal investments, there will be no Pink-Slip Blues for you."

29. When to Start Growing Your Business

THE STRONGEST MAN in Greek mythology could lift a fully-grown bull. When asked how he learned to perform that feat, he said, "I started lifting him the day he was born."

30. Shackleton's Classic Classified Ad

SIR EARNEST SHACKLETON led the first ill-fated expedition to travel completely across Antarctica in 1914. He placed the following twenty-six-word ad in the classified personal column of the London Times.

"Men wanted for hazardous journey. Small wages, bitter cold, long months of complete darkness, constant danger, safe return doubtful. Honor and recognition in case of success."

About 5,000 men applied. Shackleton picked twenty-seven and set sail just before the outbreak of World War I. They failed their mission: their ship *Endurance* became frozen into the ice pack, beginning a two-year hellish struggle to survive; including an 800 mile voyage for help in a tiny lifeboat. But Shackleton did succeed: he brought back every member of his crew, leaving no man behind.

Shackleton said he had adopted the personal motto of his father as his own: *"Find a way, or make a way."* If your own payroll checks cease, you need to remember this idea.

(I recall one $25 classified ad we wrote for a client's World Wide Web design services. It pulled in a $5,000 project from a famous tractor manufacturer).

31. Consider Toastmasters to Polish Your Style

TWO YEARS IN TOASTMASTERS CLUB was one of the best investments I ever made in myself.

When Control-O-Fax founders T. Wayne Davis and Marvin Klepfer hired me in 1961 to sell Thermo-Fax copy machines in Northeast Iowa they *suggested* I become a member of Toastmasters International Club, along with their other salesmen. They picked up the nominal dues; we paid for our own dinner meals at the monthly meetings.

The Minnesota Mining and Manufacturing Co. (3M) in the Twin Cities made the Thermo-Fax. It was the first dry process copier on the market: an infrared lamp reflected an image into a special heat-sensitive paper wherever carbon was detected. No carbon? No copy. Vegetable-based inks in ballpoint pens were our nemesis. It weighed 40 pounds and sold for $359. 'Winter, spring, summer, fall, carry the machine on every call.'

The copy zipped through in four seconds. Some office workers were astounded by the demonstrations. Copies cost a nickel for the letter-size special papers, which tended to get brittle in the files; they turned black in sunlight.

I'D TAKEN a management trainee's job with the Goodyear Service Store in Ames, IA right out of college, after working for them part time during college in Waterloo's retail store. I only had the one job interview. They offered me a job, so I took it.

Our Irish-Catholic (Before The Pill) family was growing faster than my income, so eighteen months later when a college pal told me what he was earning selling Thermo-Faxs, I interviewed with Mr. Marvin Klepfer.

"Are there any other dry copiers on the market," I asked.

Marvin took his usual long, deliberate draw on his pipe before he answered in an exhale of thick smoke:

"There is one outfit by the name of Haloid, up in Rochester, New York that has some monstrosity thing they're trying to rent for $95 *per month* plus a nickel per copy. I wouldn't worry about them if I were you, it's too expensive."

Haloid's copier turned out to be the Model 914, which became the single most profitable machine, of any kind, of all time. It cost $2,400 to manufacture, but the average annual rental eventually turned out to be $5,000 per year for ten years. Do the math.

Haloid changed their name later that year to XEROX.

I BELIEVE THE SELF-CONFIDENCE gained at Toastmasters Club carries over to normal day-to-day business relationships. It's a worthwhile investment even if you never address an audience.

Unlike the sledgehammer approach of some famous syndicated speaking courses costing hundreds of dollars, Toastmasters is like pleasant orthodontia: slow, steady improvement over months or years. It's cheap, and it's fun.

III: GETTING READY & GETTING PAID

You can get further with determination and dynamite, than you can with just determination; especially if your dream is to sculpt the world's biggest statue. There must be something in the water at Rapid City, SD. The Crazy Horse Memorial is just seventeen miles from Mt. Rushmore.

Mr. Korczak Ziolkowski began to sculpt this Memorial in 1948 with his wife Ruth and ten children—seven of them are *still* working on it. In the author's view, this is a monument to *DETERMINATION.*

Mr. Robert Ringer's 30-year old book, with its deliberately provocative title, it worth its weight in gold to entrepreneurs. Literally. The scales will drop from one's eyes about the simple realities of business. McCusker's son, Patrick, passed this book along to him at a critical fork in his career. One never knows where, or when, a great idea will appear. *Feed your mind.*

A great self-renewal antidote for the midlife crisis is a perfect essay entitled "How to Retire at 35" in this chapter. It was created by Marsteller PR in the mid 60s; it's still as fresh as the day it was penned.

1. Ogilvy's Favorite Headline

DAVID OGILVY (1911–1999) was the most legendary adman in the latter half of the 20th century. His first love and secret weapon—and mine—was direct mail advertising: because it's so measurable.

He said this was his favorite headline:

"Send us your dollar and we'll cure your hemorrhoids. Or keep your dollar, and keep your hemorrhoids."

2. Understand Your Wants & Needs

WHILE YOU'RE ON THE ROAD for business purposes—actually getting tired of eating steaks—your family is back home with their own wants and needs.

Somebody was always asking Beverly how she felt about my being away so much during the week, calling on the clients for the art studio.

"Oh, I don't mind" she said. "I know that Bob has his wants and needs ... and I have my lawyers and accountants."

3. Grow Where You're Planted

ROSWELL GARST AMBLED INTO our history books when, as a hybrid corn promoter and big-time farmer, he hosted Nikita Khrushchev, the head of the USSR during the Cold War, in 1959 at his farm in Coon Rapids, Iowa.

Garst was a fearless salesman for hybrid corn, nobody intimidated him. He chased the national media around his farmstead, throwing corncobs at them. Garst-Thomas Seed company was *the* big-name dog in the seed game fight while he was still kicking.

One hot summer morning, as I was leaving the checkout desk of the Holiday Inn at the Des Moines Gray's Lake location, up plows Himself, Mr. Roswell Garst of Coon Rapids. He was a broad-beamed draft horse of a man. I'd seen his photos for twenty years.

However, Father Time was plucking at his strings: his vocal chords had succumbed to the Big C. He used an electronic voice box for conversation; a jovial Darth Vader in bib overalls.

From three feet away, our eyes met.

"She's going to be a scorcher today, Mr. Garst" I said, offering my hand.

Garst mashed my fingers together with the grip of a twice-a-day milker. Ouch.

"The only advantage to being seventy-eight years old is, most days I can say I've seen it better, and I've seen it worse" he said.

I watched him go out the door to a waiting van, thinking, I shook the hand of the man, who shook the hand of Khruschev, who shook the hands of Stalin and Eisenhower; who shook the hands of Lenin, Truman and Roosevelt.

Mr. Garst died the next year in 1977, at age seventy-nine. Years later, I swapped poems with his son, Mr. David Garst.

Over the years after that, Presidents Carter, Reagan, Ford, and Bush, all drove by our home in their presidential limos, while campaigning in Waterloo, like nobles flinging coins from horseback.

Once, the Olympic Torch runner-parade rolled by; all of this only six blocks from where I graduated high school.

A safer way to grow your business when you're getting started is to grow where you're planted.

"He who stays where he is endures."—Toa

4. Your Ideas Have Value, Don't Give Them Away

THE RIGHT IDEA is a blend of imagination and reality; the right communication is a blend of visual and verbal images; the right advertising campaign is a blend of ideas and images.

The problem is, what's right?

Research will help you find the answers.

Nevertheless, *ideas* are the coin of the realm in my business. No ideas, no eat.

After a few years of taking notes for illustration and design projects, to pass along to the artists, I began to feel like the waiter taking salad orders for lunch. And in some cases, I believed I could handle the creative process as well as the clients and the artists on my end; maybe not, I wasn't sure yet.

Two events goaded me to get into the right slot.

FIRST, AT WINNEBAGO one time for a brochure project, my contact person took me into the new motor home, which was the subject of the brochure.

I stood by the driver's lush seat at the front of the vehicle, looking down the isle. "It reminds me of the old railroad cars when I was a lad selling newspapers aboard the Illinois Central … Pullman himself would love this luxury," I said.

A few months later, I was reading a national magazine. Lo and behold, a double-page spread for the same motor home, featuring a wide-angle view of a railroad conductor, and a group of passengers in turn-of-the-century costumes.

Apparently, their Twin Cities ad agency liked the idea as well as I did. Lightening Bolt Number One

SECOND, a one-lung ad agency in Sioux City asked for my ideas to help them pitch a potential new bank client.

I laid out a campaign concept of featuring real customers, in high-contrast black & white photos for testimonial newspaper ads and outdoor billboards. For this one rare instance, I even convinced the studio to do the layouts on a *speculative* basis.

I was positive the idea would break through all the mushy clutter from the other local financials.

It did.

Months later, as I drove into Sioux City, I spied a billboard with our layout concept, right down to the type styles. At the motel, I bought the local newspaper. There on page three, our dominant size ad with the same images as on the billboard. Bingo!

I called our client agency to congratulate him.

Charlie Harness was furious.

He did not get the bank account. A larger Omaha agency took home the bacon. They also took home my idea for their own use.

When all our gnashing and bitching was done, there wasn't anything we could do about it. Lawyers cost more than the profit involved.

Lightening Bolt Number Two.

THE LESSONS? First, try to zip your lip when you get those flashes of inspiration or invention. Then remember, you're operating from a position of weakness by doing work without a clear written understanding. Hope is not rewarded.

The upside for me? As David Ogilvy quotes an old verse in one of his books: *"They copied my ideas/But they couldn't copy my mind/So I left them a'sweatin' and stealin'/A year and a half behind."*

5. You're in Charge of Self-Renewal

WHEN YOU GET TO THE JOURNEYMAN stage in your craft or profession it's so easy to coast through the years. You may have *enough* money, and you're getting respect from your associates. Why rock the boat.

The following ad (reprinted by permission)—circa 1965—captured my attention long ago; you may get some whispers in your ear from it also. It was a house ad for the worldwide advertising/PR/marketing firm of Marsteller Inc. (*Note: Ladies, please, no letters; we acknowledge times have changed for the better).*

HOW TO RETIRE AT THIRTY-FIVE

It's easy.

Thousands of men do it every year. In all walks of life.

And it sets our economy, our country, and the world back thousands of years in terms of wasted resources. But worst of all is the personal tragedy that almost always results from "early retirement."

It usually begins with a tinge of boredom. Gradually a man's work begins to seem endlessly repetitive. The rat race hardly seems worth it any more. It's at this point that many a 35-year-old boy wonder retires. There are no testimonial dinners or gold watches. He still goes to work every day, puts in his forty hours, and even draws a paycheck. He's retired, but nobody knows it. Not at first, anyhow.

The lucky ones get fired in time to make a fresh start. Those less fortunate hang on for awhile—even decades—waiting and wondering. Waiting for a raise or promotion that never comes, and wondering why.

There are ways to fight back, though, and most men do. They counteract the urge to coast by running as they've never run before. They run until they get the second wind that is now known as "self renewal."

Self-renewal is nothing more or less than doing for yourself what your parents, teacher, coaches, and bosses did for you when you seemed young enough to need it. It's the highest form of self-discipline. And it can be one of the most satisfying experiences a man can enjoy.

Self-renewal is the adult's ability to motivate himself: to reawaken his self-pride in the face of spiritual fatigue.

Self-renewal is the device by which the boy wonders become men. Leaders. Creators. Thinkers.

Self-renewal is probably the greatest test a businessman must face. It's worth the effort though. With the life expectancy approaching the century mark, sixty-five years is a long time to spend in a rocking chair.

WHENEVER I READ THIS wonderful essay, it makes me wonder if I should go back to selling shoes. It takes chutzpah to put this ruby amidst my red glass.

6. Make Sure You Get Paid

TODAY, ALMOST THIRTY YEARS after it was first published, Robert J, Ringer's *Winning Through Intimidation* continues to stir debate.

The current Amazon.com website presents twenty-two customer reviews; most rate it with five stars. It's still only six bucks for the paperback.

I believe it's one in a handful of the best books in the success literature from the 20^(th) century.

Why?

I personally used Mr. Ringer's philosophy guidelines as a recipe to move from the image of 'just a salesman' at the art studio, to creating a full-service ad agency. His book is based upon Reality, not what we may wish about how the business world works. His tortoise-like images were just what I needed to crystallize my thinking.

Ringer gives exact techniques to overcome being intimidated by others: not by harming others, but knowing how to earn something of value, then maintain your grasp on whatever you've earned.

He underscored only two words in his book. Those words were burned into my psyche then, and deserve to be passed along to you here:

Get Paid.

Those may be the two most important words in this book. You decide.

Mr. Ringer's book came to me from my son Patrick at the time I decided to leave the art studio. It opened my eyes to the nuances of negotiation skills, and the major importance of having a long-term-thinking attitude.

He roundly condemns "Short-term patching" as a way to run your business—or your life.

Ringer was a real estate agent by trade, but his stories translate to any business. His main points are:

1) In Reality, people do not want to *give* you their money. You have to negotiate it from them.
2) "Don't waste your time and effort on factors that are not Relevant to your earning, and receiving income. Simple, but important; simple, but practiced by very few people."
3) It's not what you say or do that counts; it's your position when you say or do it. It's those written understandings in your files that count.
4) The way to be more efficient is to work on bigger deals. i.e. would you prefer 10 percent of a thousand dollars or a million dollars?
5) Successful people in business have a powerful 'intimidating' image. Their power is based upon money, legal agreements, and finally on their ability to perform what they promise.

RINGER HAD BEEN DOWN and out, so he decided that since he didn't have the money, he would substitute *guts*.

Then, he developed written agreements that could withstand 'Legalman,' the lawyers who always pop up in real estate deals.

Finally, he added a heavy, lush introductory brochure with a photo of the planet on the cover.

He vowed to perform his services so thoroughly, nobody could ever question whether he had earned his commission fees. i.e. what he called 'Performance Power.'

In his book he tells funny stories about getting screwed, learning from his experience, then later forgetting some of his lessons of pain, and getting screwed again. Why can't we ever learn from pleasure?

In the end, he made a ton of money and had a great time. He published several other books, but none with the simple truth and charm, plus the provocative title of this first one.

I've only highlighted Ringer's book here, but it provided the last cornerstones of correct knowledge needed for the foundation to erect our own future business upon.

Although, a business of our own was the last thing I ever wanted again. *I was the reluctant entrepreneur.* I was like Mark Twain's cat that'd sat on a hot stove: that cat never wanted to sit on another hot stove, but he wouldn't sit on a cold one either.

7. AIDA and The Naked Maples

MR. ROBERT RINGER knew the word 'Intimidation' in his book title, *Winning Through Intimidation,* would upset people. It's deliberately provocative and attention getting.

However, the sales process depends upon getting the prospect's attention. Once Ringer has your attention he may be able to persuade you to his point of view with the rest of his philosophy.

No attention, no sale. No sale, no eat.

There's a timeless acronym, which has served me well over the years, to help remember the usual steps to getting the order—and most important—getting paid.

AIDA ... the lady's name: ***Attenton, Interest, Desire and Action***.

It works in personal selling, public relations work and in all forms of advertising communication.

Be honest now. Did the word 'Naked' in the heading above get your attention?

BUT WAIT, YOU SAY. Why do we have to be so cynical and manipulative? Does one have to become a cold schemer to be a success in the business world?

No, you don't.

If you maintain your sense of humor. If you can remember it's all a game, to see whom can end up with the most chips at the end. It's not life or death.

That was the redeeming, charming element in Mr. Ringer's book. He added his 'Ice Ball theory,' which states that the world is going to become an ice ball in a million years due to global warming.

So, why worry?

Don't take our little game of business too seriously. Life is short. Have fun with your work. Take your vacations. Go on Spring Break. Release and relax.

The "pursuit of happiness" clause is in our Declaration of Independence. Put it in yours.

In our culture, workaholics deserve their own twelve-step program. That's why 'Carpe Diem'—seize the day—is always a popular genre for verse.

AS PART OF MY NEWFOUND long-term thinking strategy, we surrounded our old two-story duplex with Norway maple trees to provide cooling-effect shade.

These trees are like children; they grow faster than you think. When they began to reach above my second floor office windows, they inspired these St. Patrick's Day verses.

THE NAKED MAPLES

The naked maples seemed to lean
　　toward a southeast sunrise.
Their bare stiff limbs eager for
　　warm kisses upon cold thighs.

My roses were sleeping as the dawn
　　crept up earlier each day.
"Wake up!" the cardinal sang while
　　traces of snow melted away.

My thawing mind-body whispered,
　　"Time for St Paddy's fling.
Time for sport, time for fishing,
　　goodbye winter, hello spring."

When spring beckoned at my window,
    did I go out and play?
Or wait till autumn plucked my ear,
    "Goodbye, this is your last day."

Now, the naked maples lean on me;
    my grave's a cold crowded place.
No room for sport that I can see,
    my future's in my face.

8. Marketing: 101.5

WHEN I WAS IN COLLEGE, McDonald's started out selling their basic hamburgers for fifteen cents. Today, they claim to serve forty-five million customers a day worldwide.

In that same period of time our dominant industry shifted from Steel to Entertainment; from Pittsburgh and Detroit to Hollywood and Nashville.

Perhaps we became a drive-through *'Fast Food Nation'* due to the way our college graduates are trained to think:
Science Degree graduates ask, "Why does it work?"
Engineering graduates ask, "How does it work?"
Accounting graduates ask, "What will it cost?"
Marketing graduates ask, "You want fries with that?"

(Frozen french fries cost .30 lb., then the fast food
trainees heat them in vegetable oil to sell at $6 lb.).

9. Accounting: 101.5

IF YOU ASK A BOOKKEEPER what two and two is, he'll say, "I think the answer is probably four."

Ask an accountant the same question, she'll say it's positively, absolutely four."

Ask any CPA the same question, they'll walk over to the window, close the blinds and whisper "What do *you* want it to be?"

10. Seek Unvarnished Advice, Second & Third Opinions

RESIGNING THE STUDIO: Indeed, this time there would be no quick fixes. I was determined to ___think long-term___. Ten years. Twenty-five years. How did I want to spend the rest of my working days?

My first goal was to work into a Waterloo-Metro area advertising agency. But, nothing was available to me.

My second objective was to be more efficient by working on bigger deals.

Maybe I should look outside of advertising?

The real estate market was hot. Some of my high school pals were making a bundle. It seemed that real estate licenses were being scattered from airplanes. Anybody could pick one up from the sidewalk and start earning big money.

However, why fool around with ninety thousand-dollar residences when I'm surrounded with million dollar F-A-R-M-S. Lots of them. Iowa has about 100,000 farms. The 1970's inflation had puffed up the agriculture land value bubble.

I was going to do my research this time. I located a prominent farm realtor in Mason City, Iowa. He sounded a bit puzzled when I called for a luncheon appointment at his convenience, but he then set the time and place.

I WAVE TO HIM across the motel dining room. We introduce ourselves, then go through the buffet lunch.

He's about twenty-five years older than I am. A polished professional in expensive casual dress, which he can wear anywhere in town or country. Tan and thicker through the middle, he's built for comfort.

I'm looking a real pro in the eyes, over our chicken and salad couisine.

I explain my present situation—thinking about getting into his business—but certainly no competitive threat to him. What's his opinion of that idea?

"Bob" he said, "I was once young and handsome like you, believe it or not. And I had a family to think about too. So, I'll try to steer you straight.

"Have you ever sold to farmers?" he asked.

"No" I answered.

"How long do you think it would take to get established with farmers in your home-base area?" he asked.

"Couple years, probably" I answered.

"Bob, how long have you been in your present business?"

"Five years all together, with the studio and A-Mark" I replied.

"Can you pick up the phone and m-a-k-e m-o-n-e-y?" he asked.

"Well … yes, I guess I can, when you put it that way," I said.

"Bob, your customer relationships are your greatest asset. Don't take them lightly. You'll be tossing all that away if you switch fields again, regardless of the size of the deals.

"Maybe you should look for bigger deals in your advertising business," he said.

This was long before we started using today's wonderful American expression, spelled D-u-h-!

WE SHOOK HANDS in the parking lot. He drove off. That was the only time I ever saw or talked to him. However, his words have marched down through the decades with me like fellow Marines.

"Can you pick up the phone and make money?"

"Yes, Sir! Thank you for reminding me, Sir."

His willingness to help me was an act of kindness. I've tried to pass it along over the years.

I'd regained more confidence in my business judgement again. I'd remembered to do the smart thing: get an outside expert's unbiased, unvarnished opinion on a critical issue.

For a third—insider's biased—opinion, I had the advantage of being married to a radio and television station staff person. Beverly was in her fifth year at Blackhawk Broadcasting. She had a perspective from the larger corporate world, which was valuable in guiding my decision making process.

Eventually, I resigned the studio and joined the Des Moines-based Graphic Center as VP of Marketing. During my five-year stint there, I sold and created complete projects under one roof: Copy, design, photography, printing and some print advertising. I was able to keep living in Waterloo, and continue to do business with many of my previous clients.

They say it takes forty years for a walnut tree, and a man, to mature. There may be some truth to that.

11. Crazy Horse & Keeping Your Eyes on the Prize

MR. EARL NIGHTINGALE had focused upon determination in his speeches. He said you could take everything away from a good man except his family, and he'd come back strong in a year or two.

The success books of the 20th century are filled with stories of persistence and perseverance. You'll find tales, which inspire you to keep your eyes on the prize.

Remember, it's more important to know where you want to go, than how to get there. You'll find a way.

Consider the history of cathedral building, like the Chartres Cathedral in Chartres, France to inspire long-term goal thinking. That sort of construction was fostered by an institution, the Catholic Church; it was completed by 600 years of non-union builders.

THERE IS A STORY of one man's determination you may not be familiar with, which focuses the mind; it's about something going on here in the USA.

Mr. Korczak (pronounced 'Corjock') Ziolkowski was born in Boston in 1908, then orphaned at age one.

At sixteen he fled a brutal guardian to become a prominent sculptor by age 31. He won a first prize at the 1939 World's Fair for his bust of Paderewski, the great Polish pianist and statesman.

In 1941—Joe Dimaggio's hitting streak, Ted Williams batting .406, infamous Pearl Harbor—Korczak went to Rapid City, South Dakota to meet a new client.

Standing Bear, a chief of the Sioux Indian nation asked Korczak to carve a memorial to Crazy Horse in the Black Hills.

Korczak often said there was a parallel between the Native Americans and the Polish people as far as their history was concerned: i.e. frequently invaded, always getting screwed.

Korczak enlisted in the Army for World War II and served in Europe. He thought about Crazy Horse, then decided to do the memorial—not a tourist attraction—when he returned in 1947 with $174 in his pocket.

He selected a 6,000-foot mountain only seventeen miles down the road from Mount Rushmore. In 1948 the first dynamite blast brought down ten tons of rock from Thunderhead Mountain.

In 1950 Korczak married Ruth, he was 42, she was 24. They had five boys and five girls. Seven of the children are *still* working on the project.

Korczak turned down federal aid, saying he knew of 300-plus treaties the government made with the Indians—then violated. He was also aware of the hassles Borglum, the Rushmore sculptor, had endured from the Feds.

In 1982 Korczak died. He is buried at the foot of his sculpture. He had single-handedly raised millions of dollars to keep the work going, with his family in charge.

He left notebooks of instructions for them to follow. Nine people are working full-time on it today. His wife told of how so many people hate Monday mornings, but how lucky she is to have spent her life doing work she loves, and can be proud that she's done her best.

For this world's largest statue they have moved over nine million tons of rock so far, compared to 500,000 tons for Rushmore in sixteen years.

It will stand 563 feet tall—by design—eight feet higher than the Washington Monument. It will be 641 feet long. A ten-story building could fit into the opening under Crazy Horse's arm, and all four faces on Rushmore could fit inside his head. His outstretched arm will be 263 feet long, his pointing finger will be thirty-seven feet long; his hand will be thirty-three feet thick. The head of his horse will rise 219 feet from the base of the mountain; about the height of a 21-story building.

The Crazy Horse Memorial Foundation, crazyhorse.org., has adopted the slogan, 'Never Forget Your Dreams.' Their dream will take at least another determined fifty years at their current rate. Fifty Years—now that's determination.

If you want to Break Free and grow your own business, don't cut corners; take your time, do it right, think long term; remember, you become what you think about.

12. How's Your Ability to Deal With People?

"PROFESSIONALISM AND POLISH oil the wheels of Commerce; they support morale, productivity, and profitable relationships in the marketplace," said Ms. Leticia Balderidge in her *Complete Guide to Executive Manners.*

Her section on communications has been helpful for our agency business correspondence.

Professionalism does separate the wheat from the chaff; it's been on my private list of reminders for a long time.

However, there's another type of oil, which really lubricates the wheels of commerce: *Small Talk.*

The most revered business leaders I've known always took the time to ask about our children, our hobbies, even the weather and current events before launching into the business at hand.

Maybe it just gives us a chance to catch our breath, but it's refreshing, and endears the other person to us.

It's like the few extra pages at the front of a book, before a reader digs into the main course. A wooing of the reader, listener, or audience, if you will.

Fun example: James Brady, Ronald Reagan's press secretary, once impishly began taking questions at a news conference for crusty White House reporters with, "What ever happened to foreplay?"

It's impossible to put a value on Small Talk, but it's a part of the most important aspect of business success: the ability to deal with people. Why ignore it?

13. A Few Basic Ways to get New Customers: The Lifeblood of Business

GROWING A BUSINESS requires gaining new customers: the lifeblood of any business. When I joined The Graphic Center, all of my time was devoted to this endeavor. Many of these accounts had done business with me in the past, so that was the easy part.

How do you go about organizing your sales *tactics* to support your strategy of Concentration X Repetition = Effectiveness for new business?

A. Prioritize Your Prospects: Customers, Hot Prospects, Back Burner types. Then invest your time and resources accordingly. Stay in touch with those Back Burner types to replace some of today's customers who evaporate through natural attrition.

B. Organize Your Presentation: Ethos, Pathos, Logos. Aristotle's essay on *Rhetoric* defines these Greek words for persuasion techniques, according to Mortimer J. Adler, (died 2001, at age 98) as follows:

Ethos is character. You need to reveal your company's character to establish credibility with your target audience. i.e. who we are, what we do, and how we do it. This is also a simple formula for a company brochure.

Pathos is emotion. In selling, there is no substitute for enthusiasm. Remember what I told you about hiring salespeople? Look for energy, honesty and enthusiasm.

You need to arrange your sales message to appeal to the prospect's emotions.

Logos is logic. Tell them the reasons why your product or service is a fine investment. This is usually the easiest part to figure out.

Piece these three concepts together, and you'll have a powerful presentation.

Mr. Harold Geneen put together ITT, one of the first corporate conglomerates. He was also a hellava salesman. He advised his people to sell this way:

➢ Never make your sales pitch right away. Sit down with the prospect and talk about the benefits of your product.
➢ Listen to the prospect. Don't interrupt.
➢ Pick out their main objection or doubt and focus your sales talk on that.
➢ Finally, before you leave, remember to ask for the order.

C. Scouting Missions: The term "Cold Calling" sends chills through most salespeople, including me.

However, with the right frame of mind it can be an effective tool.

Treat cold calls as *scouting missions*: travel light, don't try to sell anything. Just get the right person's name to contact later. It's a great way to eyeball the potential for business that can't be gained with a phone call approach.

And you may spot your competitor's tracks.

D. Letter-Telephone-Letter: One of my successful techniques for new business is the letter-telephone call-letter campaign. Obtain your list of prospect's names from scouting, directories, referrals, direct mail, trade shows, membership lists or other means.

On Mondays, mail brief personal notes on letterhead with a introductory brochure telling the prospects you'll call later in the week, to see if they're interested.

On Wednesdays and Thursdays, call the prospects to arrange an appointment at their convenience.

This is like panning for gold in an intelligent way.

I keep two numbers on my list of reminders, which inspire me to keep at it when I'm in a new business mode: 714 and 1,330. Babe Ruth hit 714 home runs, while he struck out 1,330 times.

One of my greatest four-baggers was our Lattner Boiler Company account. While at Graphic, I found them listed in a manufacturer's directory in 1979; my letter-telephone call-letter yielded an appointment.

Steve Junge, Lattner's CEO, needed a new brochure. He's been a wonderful client for over twenty years now.

So, if you want to be self-made, get out of your office once in a while and sell your-self. Scouting and networking will help you stay current, gain new insights into your customers and competition.

14. Use Economists & Consultants Sparingly

THEY'RE BOTH EASY TARGETS: If all the Economists in the world were laid end to end, it would probably be a good idea ... An economist is a fellow without enough charisma to be an actuary.

And ... Two tomcats had been out all night on the town. As they were heading home, they jumped over backyard fences as shortcuts to beat the first rays of the sun rising in the east.

Unfortunately, the older tomcat—apparently he'd lost some spring in his step—didn't quite clear the last fence: A-G-O-N-Y, he caught the family jewels on the fence, and lost a tomcat's most treasured possessions.

"Oh my goodness (sure, that's what he said) what will I ever do now?" he screeched.

The young tomcat purred, "Don't worry, you can always be a consultant."

IV: GAINING BROADER PERSPECTIVES

What you are doing is one side of the ledger, what the Economy is doing is the other side. Why and how to keep an eye on the big picture.
Here are some accounts the author uncovered during severe recessions.

Directing the photo shoot with the model for this Fox River Mills cover was a tough job, but somebody had to do it. McCusker volunteered. Really.

Below: After finding Howe Engineered Sales in a state man-ufactures directory, the author was able to create his first national campaign for a full product line. This ad borrows from a popular 1950s women's permanent wave slogan, "Which Twin Has the Toni."

Mr. Duane Wessels, maker of these hog houses was a master marketer who keep a plastic pig named 'Jasper' on his desk. He tied a ribbon around Jasper's neck to remind himself that 'without a ribbon it's bare.'

15. Recessions: 'Money Makes Iron Float'

WHAT YOU'RE DOING is one side of the ledger. What the Economy is doing is the other side.

Why learn to keep an eye on the big picture and long term trends? There have been six recessions in the last thirty-three years. Averages: Depth -2.7% of GNP; Duration eleven months; Jobless rate 7.8% (Source: *Wall Street Journal*)

The worst downturn—10.8% unemployment—occurred when Mr. Paul Volker, central banker Federal Reserve Chairman, raised interest rates steeply in October 1979.

I remember vividly when I heard the news: where I was eating lunch, who I was with, and the sudden insight that Volker had "taken away the inflation punchbowl," and times were going to get really tough for our agribusiness clients, plus all of the farmers in the USA.

It was time to brace ourselves, and hang onto what we already had; not the time for expansion or job-hopping.

"Don't insult the alligator until you've crossed the river."

How did I *know* that, at that moment? Because I had given myself a vigorous study course in Economics over the prior three years.

I'd invested time in myself again. After my usual winter weekly Saturday visits to the Nonfiction New Books shelf, I scooped up lots of the "dismal science" economics genre from that thinly populated section.

I learned from the diminutive Milton Friedman, and others, there would be about a two year lag from the reduction in the money supply, followed by the crunch of mortgage forecloses, and the eventual leveling or falling of the inflationary farmland prices.

He was dead-on right. By 1981, it was time to bring in Willie Nelson's FARM-AID fundraisers, to lament all the white crosses erected on the Courthouse lawns across the USA. It was a Great Depression for rural folks.

Joblessness created the Midwest "Rust Belt."

Folks left my hometown for Texas and the desert southwest. It'd take us fifteen years to get our population back.

Recessions change our attitudes from risk taking to risk aversion. Pocketbooks snap shut. Cash is King.

Actually, the top one third of all the farmers just rolled over their federally insured, high-interest bearing Certificates of Deposit, while they nodded sympathetically during Sunday prayers at church for the bottom one third of farmers who were going bust.

Then they proceeded to buy their neighbor's land at 40 percent less the following year.

My brother, Bill, likes to quote the old Indian saying, *"Money makes iron float."*

IN ROUGH TIMES, the "Positive Thinking" industry cranks up to put on seminars for sales people. Books are published with ways to live more frugally. Oracles are sought out, gurus are in.

Graphic sent us all to a seminar in Des Moines. The speaker was making the point that "It all depends on the current situation, as to what actions and decisions are best."

"Imagine that I lay a plank down here on the floor: it's 12" wide, 2" thick and 10' long. If I offered you ten dollars to walk that plank, how many would do it?" he asked.

300 hands shot up.

"Now" he said, "if I take that same plank up ten stories to the top of this hotel, and stretch it across to the next building, how many would walk across the plank?"

A dozen hands went up. "See" he said, "it depends doesn't it?"

"Finally," he says, "if we have the same situation, but I'm over on the other building holding your child, and threatening to throw your child down ten stories, how many of you would walk across the plank to save your child."

I yelled out *"Which kid is it?"*

When the pandemonious laughter finally subsided, the speaker recovered cleverly, *"See, it does depend!"*

YOUR FAMILY-BASED lifestyle business may be operating under the radar, but the tides of economic forces shouldn't be totally ignored. Every once in a while, a tsunami rolls in without warning: Events like September Eleventh are beyond rational thinking.

THE WALL STREET JOURNAL is a fine investment for any businessperson; or it's free at the Public library if your cash is tight. After a few years of reading the WSJ, you'll tune your antennae for trouble—and opportunity—even if you never own a stock or bond.

Feed your mind, feed your mind, feed your mind.

"Whether you face the best of times ... or the worst of times ... they're the only times you've got."

—Art Buchwald, 1980

16. Some of My Graphic Center Entrepreneurial Clients

DURING MY FIVE YEARS working and learning with the Graphic Center, I had the pleasure of serving some of the most successful companies in the world—many of them Fortune 500 members.

I'll name some of the Big Boys here, but this is only a partial list: Amana, Maytag, Deere & Company, Meredith, Heilman Brewing, Trane Company, Fisher Controls, Ertl Toy, Oster Communications and the Mayo Clinic at Rochester, Minnesota.

I can't remember being the real leader on any of the projects we did for those big organizations. Most of their creative work is done in-house, or by their Ad agencies; we were only doing the printing or photography. But I was able to collaborate a few ideas on the work as it went through the Graphic Center.

However, I am proud of the work we did for a lot of smaller companies, where I was the prime creative force in creating their marketing tools.

IMT and HENKEL CONSTRUCTION

Mr. Daryl J. Greiman was the advertising manager for Iowa Mold Tooling at Garner, Iowa; one of those odd, minor, small-town operations that mushrooms, then outgrows its name, all due to a dynamic entrepreneural leader: Mr. Francis Zrostlik.

IMT started out converting OEM truck chassis into tire-repair fleet service trucks, for large farm tractors and heavy construction machines. Then they added boom-type-articulating cranes for construction.

Daryl is one of the most interesting men I've ever known as a good personal friend. He grew up in rural north central Iowa, then lived in Greece, while working for a construction company.

He did scuba diving and underwater photography in the Aegean Sea. A widely traveled, well read gentlemen, he is an excellent copywriter, layout designer and outstanding photographer: a triple threat.

Today, he's growing his own family-based lifestyle business in his tiny hometown of Garner: The Final Frame Shop. There's always time for golf when I call.

Mr. Zrostlik snapped him up when Daryl returned to his roots, as I had done about the some time. We did mainly printing projects for Daryl, but over many fascinating lunches, we compared ideas for all kinds of advertising techniques and copywriting concepts.

Daryl was also an avid tennis buff, and member of the Mason City—*"River City" in the Music Man musical*—Racquetball Club.

The Henkel Construction Company constructed the Club. Henkel's marketing person, a bit younger man, Tom Schaefer, played tennis with Daryl.

Tom asked his tennis pal to recommend someone to create Henkel's new corporate capabilities brochure.

"Bob McCusker is your man," said Daryl.

Mr. Thomas R. Schaefer and I have had a trusting business relationship plus a great friendship ever since, over twenty-five years.

When Tom's gentlemanly father, Mr. Rube Schaefer, passed away, Tom became president and CEO of this now much larger construction outfit.

As Professor Harold Hill, of *The Music Man* would say, "Tom has done a *Swell* job of team building, in a top-quality company, founded in 1892."

Over the years, we've done Henkel's logo, several major brochures, direct mail, video, website, and an identity package for INDIANHEAD, an immense local 300-acre commercial and industrial development.

Let others sell for you; all you have is your reputation.

Word of Mouth is always the most effective form of advertising, both good and bad. Give your customer an estimate for the business, then never, never, never exceed it.

If your credit rating is the Golden Goose, your reputation for competence and integrity is worth your weight in diamonds.

TRIANGLE PLASTICS

My first complete writer-producer responsibility was a corporate capabilities, image brochure for Triangle Plastics of Winthrop, Iowa near Waterloo.

Mr. James L. Blin, the founder and owner, attended a new products tradeshow in Des Moines. He liked Graphic's portfolio so he gave us the project.

Jim had moved his company into Winthrop because the local business leaders invested seed money, to help create hundreds of jobs, and maintain their town's vitality.

Vitality is Jim's middle name. His other names are *Energy, Honesty, and Enthusiasm.* He puts his heart and soul into everything he does—including race-cars.

Triangle is a plastics thermoformer: they take a flat sheet of plastic, stick it into a hot form, vacuum the air out to shape the plastic around the shape of the desired product. Presto! Tractor cab tops, golf cart roofs, truck bumpers, dashboard panels; for companies like Caterpillar, Deere, Yamaha.

Jim's son, Randy, and I were collaborators on many marketing projects over the years, as these dynamic entrepreneurs diversified into house shutters, and wide-turn signals for eighteen-wheelers.

I worked on their account with Graphic, then the agency that hired me next, and finally with our own agency.

HOWE ENGINEERED SALES

Take an imaginary trip with me. After I found this prospect in the state-manufacturing directory, after the Letter-Telephone-Letter tactic, I drove down Pearl Street in Cedar Falls, Iowa. I was looking for a company that marketed motorcycle accessories.

However, there was a school over there, and this was a residential neighborhood. What was in that whitewashed cinderblock structure? The address was correct. I actually thought I must be mistaken.

I don't remember why Mr. Carl Howe located his business there, but there he was assembling Cycolac ABS thermoformed—that word sounds familiar—plastic motorcycle accessories: fairing windshields, saddlebags and hauler-trailers.

I began salivating, when I realized how all of Graphic's services could give his product line the sex appeal required to compete with the market leaders.

Mr. Howe was an ex-John Deere tractor engineer; hence the unusual name for his company.

He'd started with the hauler-trailer for his own personal use as an avid touring biker. One thing led to another, he quit Deere and found suppliers—including Triangle Plastics—then began selling nationwide.

Unfortunately, he'd ripped off the Big Boy's brandname, which was "Windjammer." Carl called his products "Windkutter;" a little too close for legal comfort, in my opinion.

I believed it was only a matter of time before before Robert Ringer's "Legalman" would be knocking on his door.

I flew down to Houston with Carl for his industry's biggest trade show of the year. His competition, the Vetter Company's Windjammer, was owned by a charismatic *Easy Rider* type by the name of Mr. Craig Vetter.

The names Vetter and Windjammer were synonymous in the buyer's mind. Like Ford Mustang.

After a long day in the AstroDome tradeshow, I slept poorly. But I *dreamt* that Carl should change his brandname to "Kutter." Shorten the Windkutter to avoid legal hassles, and echo the "Vetter" sound.

I proposed the idea to Carl at breakfast. He was so excited he could have eaten his tie right along with his scrambled eggs and not noticed.

We flew back home, did a complete makeover of logo, product stripings; we did juicy outdoor location photography, new brochures and ads. Our staff had a ball with these "guy" products. I was totally involved with a national marketing plan for the first time.

I swear, Mr. Howe actually *hugged me*, when we delivered his new brochures in time for the next major show. Sales were strong. He had a clear path ahead.

A few years later, the motorcycle companies—Honda, Kawasaki, others—began installing the optional accessories as OEM standards.

TROUBLES. The aftermarket dried up.

Vetter saw the handwriting on the wall and sold out in time, but his buyer soon went belly up.

Then, tragedy struck the Howe family.

After numerous spills on his motorcycle, barely escaping the grim reaper, Mr. Howe, and his brother, were both killed in an automobile crash in rural Iowa.

Carl was the first of many to give me free rein in planning how to spend his money. Did I make some mistakes? Sure. But now, as then, we invest our client's money *very, very, very* carefully.

Carl Howe was a fun guy and a great client. I miss him, may he rest in peace.

DODGER SHORTS & MORE

Mr. Richard Ritter, now there's a tall drink of water. He allowed me to call him "High Pockets." He truly took a Main Street athletic goods store and built it into a national supplier of leisurewear clothing. Hundreds of jobs were created in his home base of Eldora, Iowa and several adjacent communities.

Dick's easy going, high-energy zest for life is apparent to everyone. His tall, lanky frame allowed him to look all of the jocks in the eye.

The foundation of Dodger Industries was built upon those drab, gray athletic shorts all the boys had to wear in gym class so long ago. Then, Dick started making every kind of shorts the jocks and coaches wanted.

And then sweat shirts and pants became socially acceptable for Grandma to wear to the new mall. Dick bought the sewing equipment and hired the farmer's wives to keep up with the Fitness & Leisure boom.

I got involved with the Dodger catalog, first at the design level, then with Graphic, where we did the entire job; selecting the models, the photography and printing. I also did a few trade ads as Dick kept expanding the product line for all types of leisurewear as that trend escalated.

Mr. Richard Ritter is a natural-born leader and a vigorous businessman of the highest integrity. He's retired from Dodger Industries now.

If there's a Hardin County Hall of Fame, he deserves a high place of honor. Anybody that can turn gray gym shorts into a mammoth stack of greenbacks has my admiration for life; you've got to love him.

POWERS ATHLETIC UNIFORMS

Horse collars? Can you believe it, this company which started in 1902, actually stitched together Langford's Humane Horse Collars in Waterloo, Iowa.

They still have their corporate headquarters in the same building on Sycamore Street.

Powers leveraged their needle skills into World War I Army canteen and wagon covers; also canvas water bags, hats and dusters for the new horseless carriage drivers.

Then they made the first black-and-white referee shirts; they developed and sold to Cluet-Peabody the "Sanforized" pre-shrinking process for men's dress shirts.

Not until 1929 did they really find their niche.

Powers invested in knitting machines and inventory for athletic wear and uniforms.

Athletic uniforms. *Real athletic uniforms,* for The Bigs: NBA, NFL, NHL, Major League baseball, colleges, high schools, and down the line. Their stuff feels like the big time, and it is. They also supply Nike.

Mr. "Ham" Weidner took over management from Mr. Powers in 1953. He was a very kindly man and generous with his time for me, so Graphic was able to produce some of his catalogs and brochures.

When our agency created the *Cedar Valley Entrepreneurs of the Century* calendar, I selected Mr. Powers as one of the honorees.

FOX SOX

Fox River Mills was another homerun account for me. Again, the state-manufacturers directory led me to their door. They are tucked away in the north central town of Osage, Iowa. The Lessard family business moved there from the Fox River Valley of Wisconsin when a fire burned down their knitting operation, which began in 1900.

Fox River makes the best damn wool socks and mittens you can wear. Bar none. Their biggest competitor, Wig Wam, may be better known to consumers.

Ms. B. J. Douglas was their marketing coordinator.

She arranged my presentation with Messieurs John and Jeff Lessard. We hit it off well and went on to do many catalogs, brochures and trade ads. I attended the main Chicago trade show to talk to their retailers.

Fox River offers a complete line of socks for all the winter sports, athletic sports, and heavy duty socks for working folks.

This was another account that stayed with me when I moved into the agency business. We did new packaging, catalogs and more trade ads.

Everything was going smoothly until Wig Wam's ad agency Account Executive started *his* own agency. He had lots of experience and trade contacts to offer the Lessards, so I certainly understood when they moved their account to his new shop.

Clients come, clients go. In the end, all we have is each other.

HYDROTILE MACHINERY

Where do roadway drainage culverts come from? Well, somebody has to have a humongus machine to mix, then pour wet concrete into forms, which produce road culverts, and all sorts of concrete pipe, even big enough for a tall man to stand in upright.

If you're in the business of producing concrete pipe, you may own a packer-head machine made by the Hydrotile Co. in Nashua, Iowa.

Nashua is more famous for being the home of The Little Brown Church in the Vale.

I worked with Hydrotile's sales manager, Mr. William Montgomery, on complex sales literature and full-page trade ads for *Modern Concrete*. Bill hailed from *"Alabama!"* and was the coolest international industrial sales type I ever knew.

Bill told me that minutes after he checked out of the Hilton Hotel in Beirut, Lebanon, it was shelled by artillery fire as his plane climbed out of that war-torn hellhole. Watching his still-warm bed being blown to bits, he decided to change his travel plans. He landed in Athens, and then he flew on to a quiet Greek Island.

Wild Bill bought a large bottle of whiskey, sat down on the beach, drank half the whiskey while pondering his fate, and gratefully watched the sun go down.

The next day, he did the same thing. Then he went back to work.

Mr. Montgomery was a delight to work with. He allowed me to do my first full-page trade ads in an editorial style. i.e. looks like a news feature with long copy, without the "world's greatest" hyperbole. I discovered that I really enjoy taking complex products and reducing their features to plain-English benefits.

Hydrotile is now out of business for a host of reasons. Bill Montgomery, I hope, is probably bass fishing on one of those north Alabama man-made lakes; maybe sipping some Tennessee home-brew.

The Little Brown Church in The Vale?

Still cranking out fresh brides and grooms almost every day. Apparently, Love is a more lasting business than concrete pipe machines.

WESSELS CONFINEMENT

My greatest weakness during this period was having the correct knowledge of Agribusiness, the key industry in my home state.

I was raised in town, so I rarely set foot on a farm. This is true of most Iowans, contrary to our Grant Wood, "American Gothic" image.

When I was born in 1935, one in four Americans lived on a farm. Now, it's two out of a hundred.

My weakness was brought into focus while I was still with the art studio. Through serendipity, I had the opportunity to create a double-page, full color, farm magazine advertising spread for a major seed company.

We were creating a seed guide for them, and the ad project just fell into my lap.

I went over to the studio on a Sunday night. It was quiet enough so I could do the rough layout and write the copy without distractions.

I was able to arrange the photos, but then I was stuck. No words. I didn't have clue how to talk to farmers.

We finally cobbled together something that *looked* good enough, but I knew I was up the creek on Agribiz accounts.

When I joined Graphic I was able to start learning about agribusiness marketing. I joined NAMA, the National Agribusiness Marketing Association.

Their regular meetings around the state featured members speaking about their strategy and tactics.

Graphic had a great roster of Ag clients; the most prominent was PIONEER SEED. I was able to study our printing samples for their products to gain the insight and trade jargon for farmers.

The farmer is probably the most researched critter on earth. Their numbers are dwindling; their average age keeps rising, so the trend will continue.

Incidentally, they prefer to be called farmers, not producers.

MR. DUANE WESSELS HAD NINE LIVES in the livestock confinement buildings business. Those are the buildings, which are used for factory-like production of your bacon-and-eggs breakfast.

When I had the pleasure of first calling on Mr. Wessels, we conducted our meeting with him sitting on an empty five-gallon can in his still-under-construction office. He gave me his only chair.

Mr. Wessels is one of the most *charming* men I've ever known. Sell iceboxes to Eskimos? No problem. He could talk a dog off from a meat truck.

When I met this serial entrepreneur he was starting his umpteenth agribusiness venture. He called it ILS for International Livestock Systems.

Duane was building prefabricated modular units, for delivery down the highway onto the farmer's foundation, with the obligatory pit dug underneath for the you-know-what.

Duane's concept was to build solar panels into the roof of the units: Solar-Sist Confinement Systems.

Did the panels work? Somewhat. At times.

Duane kept a little plastic pig sitting on his desk. He called him "Jasper." Jasper looked just like any other pig, except Duane had tied a ribbon around his neck. "Because without a ribbon it's bare."

Duane's marketing prowess was being able to find a ribbon to tie on anything.

He was so well known personally in the confinement segment of the market, I convinced him to name his company, WESSELS, Inc., to market Wessels Solor Confinement Systems.

We created his logo, and the Taj Mahal of corporate brochures: full color, double-gate-fold to 40" wide, die-cut, blind-embossed, 12-point KromeKote enamel cover stock with a flap inside to hold proposals … All to sell *hoghouses.*

Then I convinced him to paint his logo on the ends of those buildings in *three-foot high letters,* so farmers driving by at 55–65 MPH could read them. Duane thought the farmer-buyer might go Postal and shoot up the factory when he saw the units roll onto his farmstead.

Not a whimper. We got away with the free advertising.

Apparently, when it came to who was the best salesman, we each had met our match.

Man, that guy can sell stuff.

Nevertheless, the hog business is notorious for boom and bust. Duane busted like lots of others during the farmland real estate bubble bust.

Mr. Wessels went on to a brilliant career in the insurance business, with all those lovely repeat commissions. Recently retired, he's active in local politics.

Remember Jasper: without a ribbon it's bare.

ROCHESTER SILOS

The Rochester Silo Company was located in Rochester, Minnesota, the hometown of the world-renowned Mayo Clinic.

So, whenever I called upon the Mayo Clinic, I made it a point to cultivate my relationship with the advertising manager at the silo manufacturer.

Mr. Stuart Dormandy was a lively, witty marketer with a pilot's license to boot; he was also the company pilot.

During the severe farm depression around 1980, Stuart sold his management on letting Graphic create the Godzilla of sales presentation binders.

Stuart supplied the photos and sales copy; we did the cut-away illustrations showing the innards of their silos.

Again, full-color printing, heavy, coated cover paper stock; three-hole punched and all housed in an elaborate, expensive *genuine leather* zipper binder. Big bucks project: Middle five figures.

During one of our many meetings over the years, Stuart said, "Bob, you sure ask a lot of questions."

"Do I?" I answered.

Did the large investment in the new sales binders help the sales force lift the company out of the farm economy depression?

No way. The farmers didn't have any money.

What you're doing is one side of the ledger; the other side is the overall economy.

17. Keep On Networking After You Bloom

WHEN THE AUTUMN LEAVES began turning colors in my first year with Graphic, I returned to the campus of my alma mater for an evening dinner meeting.

The Marketing Department of the College of Business had adopted the orphan Sales & Marketing Executives Club. The SME Club had been the center of gravity for sales types back in the early 1960's when I was selling Thermo-Fax machines. I'd earned their Distinguished Salesman Award one year.

As the Club leadership had dwindled, it morphed into a university Town & Gown professional group, with the college professors leading the way.

I still recall some of the other folks at the first meeting I attended: Don Irwin and Betty Sproule from the Colle McVoy Advertising agency; and Saul Diamond was the leader-professor from the University of Northern Iowa.

It was all very pleasant and professional cordiality was overflowing. However, as they say in Texas, it was "all hat and no cattle." Professionalised ordinariness is my recollection.

Nevertheless, my goal was to develop long-term relationships in the Waterloo/Cedar Fall area. So, I just gripped and grinned, then watched through the full season of meetings.

The following autumn I was the featured speaker at the first club meeting to introduce the Graphic Center's capabilities and spin a few war stories from my account work in the real world.

I put a lot of effort into my presentation; had a custom-made series of slides showing Graphic's work for a wide range of clients.

Parsu, the Indo-American professor who was the meeting leader that night, paid me the most endearing compliment I ever received in all my years as a speaker. "You earned a great deal of respect from your peers tonight," he said.

I was on my way locally.

By the time the May meeting rolled around the following spring, I sensed this club was on it's last legs.

The meeting was held at a local run-down motel; only fourteen people showed up. The speaker for the evening was the sales manager for a leading hog feed company.

The speaker treated his captive audience as though we were his sales force rather than professionals.

This self-winding speaker ignored his time limit and went through his four-inch stack of overhead transparencies in butt-busting detail. Mercifully, it finally ended.

Pausing in the parking lot afterward, one of the officers of the Club asked me to join the board of directors for the following year of programs.

"Charlie, it's easier of give birth than it is to resurrect the dead. This Club should be put to sleep," I said.

WHAT MAKES A CLUB THRIVE and prosper? "It's the programs, stupid," to paraphrase a political slogan.

First-class speakers must be booked long in advance. Then we'd need a direct-mail promotional program, coupled with a benign dictator to run the meetings like a Toastmaster's tight ship—namely me.

I could plainly see a vacuum for the new club patterned after the best components I'd experienced as a member and guest speaker at other advertising and marketing clubs.

I could *recognize a rich opportunity* to position myself as a leading marketing professional. It could open doors for me on neutral ground to meet the advertising agency folks I wanted to get hired by ... A chance to be in the limelight locally.

That summer I invited well-known local professionals in all areas of marketing for a luncheon meeting.

There was Don Irwin, Saul Diamond, Mike McCollum from KWWL-TV and myself. I outlined my plans for the new club: the Marketing & Advertising Club of Northeast Iowa.

We would still retain the symbiotic relationship with the University, but working professionals would be in charge.

At Nino's steakhouse that day, we gave birth to what would become know affectionately as MAC.

We elected ourselves officers. I wanted Irwin as President due to his gray-haired prominence in the agency business. I took Vice President of Programs because that's where the work had to be done; it would also give me more visibility at *every meeting*.

I would follow in the second year as President.

I wrote my check for the dues, handed it to Mike as the new treasurer. I was the number one charter member.

My plan went into gear.

I lined up nine main after-dinner speakers, plus three 15-minute, pre-dinner "Spotlight" new member speakers for each meeting. For a total of thirty-six speakers for the first full season.

I *knew* each one of those new member Spotlight speakers would bring their own audience for moral support and visibility for their companies, which of course they did.

I created a direct mail package promoting the new club with the full season of programs all complete. Dues were dirt-cheap, the dinners were reasonable.

The first meeting was held at the respectable, local Elks Club in Waterloo. Sixty-five new members attended the first meeting, including several of the agency people I was courting long-term for a position on their staff. The right offer I was seeking *would* come along at the right time.

Over the next couple of years I met some of my best friends and colleagues of today. One in particular, Dr. Steven Corbin, Professor of Marketing at UNI, is one of my most-trusted friends and confidantes in the world.

I thought I'd done a fabulous job of building MAC membership to 125 members at the end of my term as president. However, when that rascal Corbin was president, he ran it up to 250. A record that was never equaled since. That guy knows how to market.

MAC was my baby. I attended 108 meetings without an absence. By promoting MAC, I had promoted myself in the community. I was a leader and active member for sixteen years before stepping back from the club. I left it a tight, happy ship.

In recent years MAC membership has slipped below one hundred. They've raised their dues and offer fewer speakers? "*The old is forever new.*"

Maybe there's a leadership opportunity there for you to get involved?

V: HOW TO BREAK FREE

"I'd never been laid off before. It smarts. Makes your eyes water. Both Beverly and I were going to be fifty years old that year. At that moment neither of us had a full-time job. Now what?"

Robert McCusker — **Beverly McCusker**

Advertising, marketing agency opens

McCusker & McCusker, an advertising and marketing agency, recently opened for business in Waterloo.

Advertising, public relations and sales promotion will be the primary activities of the firm owned by Beverly and Robert McCusker. The agency's goals will be "to help clients get new business ... and retain present customers."

In addition to metro firms, it will also serve the Small Business Development Center at the University of Northern Iowa.

counsels small businesses in eastern Iowa.

The McCuskers are life-long Waterloo residents and have both experience in marketing and advertising. She gained broadcast experience with KWWL and McCusker has been involved in selling advertising for a variety of clients.

He is a founder and past president of the Marketing and Advertising Club of Northeast Iowa and earned a business degree.

In 1985, almost two months after their 'stealth opening' the local paper gave the 50-year old partners an above-the-fold feature on the business cover.

Below: They produced direct mail packages for the local Ad club which enhanced their reputation of effective work with a flair.
[Photographer unknown]

Don't throw out the baby with the bathwater!

Quality programming and networking opportunities may save you from throwing the baby out with the bathwater!

1. Mergers & Acquisitions

THE LION CAN LIE down with the Lamb.
However, the Lamb won't get any sleep.

~ Woody Allen

2. My Positive Kick in the Pants

MAC CLUB HELPED ME create my network of contacts in the advertising agency business.

When I'd joined the Graphic Center it was owned by two gentlemen, who also owned the biggest agency in Des Moines. However, eighteen months later, they sold Graphic to an *accountant/consultant*. Double trouble, in my opinion.

"The Piranha" was my code name for him. He chewed some edges off from my "written understanding."

But, I patiently went about my business building relationships on my side of the state. My copywriting skills were gradually getting better. MAC had produced fine visibility; I had demonstrated leadership ability and perseverance.

Then, I escaped. After five years with Graphic, the perfect offer surfaced for me. In 1982, at age 47, I resigned Graphic.

I migrated from the graphic arts business to become a "copy-contact" Account Executive for a highly respected Waterloo advertising agency: Cooper Jenner Stafford. New Business was my assignment again.

The three partners were wonderful people as well as excellent advertising and business executives; aged about sixty, fifty, and forty. All thoroughly charming professionals.

The agency employed a total of nine, including me. Their volume was robust; their attitude was growth and aggressiveness about the Midwest economy emerging from recession.

What could go wrong?

Then, four weeks after I joined the agency, Mr. Billy Jenner died suddenly from of a heart attack at age fifty.

Billy had been Mr. Volunteer in the community. His passing was a shock and a loss for all of us.

Nevertheless, my previous clients gave me the necessary business to start bringing in revenue. I was happy and healthy; I was doing work that I loved.

Beverly was approaching her tenth year at Blackhawk Broadcasting. She was on-air hostess for a five-minute television public service program. Her guests were promoting their organization's up-coming events.

Beverly's community visibility was beginning to exceed mine. (One lady approached her at the super-market to whisper, "You're getting better.")

She was also the executive secretary for two vice presidents. She was then, and is today, a rare combination of administrative competence and show-biz vitality.

Beverly's acting skills from high school were paying off, and her natural talent stirred up desires to get back on the stage before a live audience.

The following year Beverly resigned her position in broadcasting, to work only at home for a well-deserved sabbatical. She free-lanced the noontime show; they taped several at a time. She also accepted a part-time job offer doing some book-keeping for an insurance agent friend for pin money.

Then, she sneaked up on the Waterloo Community Playhouse. I've hardly seen her since. (That's a joke.)

My client list continued to grow: Triangle Plastics, Lattner Boiler, Fox Sox, Hawkeye Bank and Hoffman Seed Farms.

The economy was picking up. Returning from a meeting in Dubuque with Mr. Cooper, I recall hearing on the car radio that the Dow-Jones stock index had surged that day to a new high of 777!

Mr. Jim Stafford was the youngest partner at the agency. He'd remarried shortly after Mr. Jenner's death. However, after a year or so, he moved far away in an effort to resolve some issues from his first marriage.

The times were a'changin'.

Now, the founder, Mr. Frank Cooper was the sole owner again. When Mr. Stafford left the firm, Frank hired another senior account executive, an excellent, widely experienced man, Mr. Les Dewey. I'd known him when he was with the ACCO Seed Co., and the Federal Land Bank in Omaha, Nebraska.

In February of 1985, Beverly and I went on vacation to visit her brother Jim, and his wife Judy, in Lake Jackson, Texas. Free food and winter golf.

After our return, on Friday, March 8th, at 4:00 in the afternoon, Mr. Cooper called me into his office and closed the door. He informed me I was to be laid-off with two weeks notice. He would see what he could do to help me find another position as I continued my work at the agency.

I'd never been laid-off before. It smarts. Makes your eyes water.

Both Beverly and I were going to be fifty years old that year. At that moment neither of us had a full-time job.

Now what?

3. Pink Slip Blues? Negotiate More Time ...

IF YOU'RE LAID OFF OR DOWNSIZED you need all the time you can negotiate to get your bearings and chart a new course.

I'm aware that in today's wonderful world of 'Human Resources,' some companies walk you to the door after an hour's notice to clean out your desk.
Probably in hopes you won't go Postal on them. Nice people. Avoid that kind of
company if you can.

However, in my case I had two weeks notice from Mr. Cooper. Fair enough I
thought.

Nevertheless, the next day, on Saturday, I had the Pink Slip Blues.

And so, the following week I stopped in Des Moines to get counseling from
an old networking friend and Graphic colleague, Mr. Duane Swensen. Duane
had escaped The Piranha before I did. He'd established a catalog photography
studio, with dozens of employees.

Duane's staff had photographed the Dodger and Fox River catalogs for me. All
first-class work.

Duane suggested I make a counter-offer to Mr. Cooper: after the two weeks
notice salary period was up, to work for a flat ten bucks an hour for up to ninety days.

I'd certainly be giving up some money, but I'd still have a nice office and the
image of a successful executive, and not have to take the first offer that came
along. Great advice.

I presented my counter-offer memo to Mr. Cooper. He generously accepted:
the hourly rate was fine, but he held the time period to six weeks, making a total
of eight weeks to make my move.

It's not what you say or do, it's your position when you say or do it.—Ringer

My position had just improved tremendously. My friend Duane's "outsider's
perspective with an insider's information", gave me the confidence and moral
support when I needed it most.

4. Our Belt and Suspenders Beginnings

"WHETHER YOU'RE A LION OR A GAZELLE, when the sun comes up,
you'd better be running." When I was laid-off we had eight weeks to decide how
to spend the rest of our lives. So, I too was running for my life.

Not to sound too overly melodramatic, but I figured that I'd spent the first
twenty-five years of my life overcoming the handicaps I was born with. Then, it
took the next twenty-five years to overcome the handicaps I'd given myself.

Now, I wanted to live another twenty-five years enjoying myself. If not now, when?

"The Horses of Time gallop on the downhill side."

The good news: I wasn't a one-man band. Beverly's strength and wisdom were there to guide me this time.

This time I wouldn't make a decision, where if everything went wrong, we'd be back in a rented house, and I'd be back selling shoes again. Nevermore.

The last thing on my mind was founding another business of my own. I was the reluctant entrepreneur.

So, I picked up the phone again to make money.

I put out the word to my network of personal and professional relationships: I was looking for a position as agency account executive, advertising manager for a smaller company, adjunct professor at the University; or perhaps a permanent Community College teaching position.

I didn't breathe a word to any of the clients I was serving for the agency.

My friends at the University of Northern Iowa were the first to respond; especially, Dr. Steve Corbin, who was acting as the Head of the Marketing Department.

Steve urged me to interview with the Director of the Small Business Development Center, Mr. Al Pelham, located on the UNI campus. I knew Mr. Pelham quite well from our times breaking bread together at MAC club.

5. The Small Business Development Center

The SBDC is a free consulting service, which is a part of the Small Business Administration: the SBA.

These counseling services are free to anybody, your taxes pay for them: business plans, finance, human resources, accounting, and my bread-and-butter, marketing.

Mr. Pelham was swamped with folks starting businesses in those days. He couldn't counsel them all himself, so he referred them to outside counselors with the expertise they required, Pelham had a Federal funds budget for outside counselors, which paid for up to twenty hours of professional services per client, at about 60-percent of the local going rate.

"Are you interested in doing free-lance counseling for the SBDC?" Mr. Pelham asked.

"Well, I'm still employed by the ad agency, but I'll see what we can work out," I said.

If my concept of Risk dictated never leaving the house without a belt *and* suspenders, my Uncle Sam had just said, "Here, take my suspenders."

6. The 'Over-Qualified' Facts of Life

Over the next few weeks, I had job interviews, was told I was "over-qualified," (too old?) and earned my very first money strictly for consulting services, with a couple of "too-small-for-the-agency" clients.

Business folks said, "Here, take this money, tell me what to do." My reputation and carefully crafted image were starting to pay off at that precise moment, our proverbial fork-in-the-road. How sweet it is.

Mr. Cooper arranged for me to interview for an advertising manager's job with Mr. Bill Plantan, the CEO of J. S. Latta School Supplies, in Cedar Falls. This 100-year-old company sold mainly with their 400-page catalog and well-entrenched sales force.

My job would be to keep the catalog up-to-date and produce some sales flyers. Mr. Plantan offered me the job on the spot. I told him I'd consider it overnight.

I confessed to Beverly that a cut-and-paste future with that catalog was my worst nightmare. She sympathized, so I turned down the offer.

Sadly, Mr. Plantan died prematurely a short time later from a heart attack; the company was sold several times over by different owners. The fellow who did accept that job lasted less than a year, before escaping back into the broadcasting business.

I'd dodged a bullet.

Mr. Cooper approved the idea of me doing some SBDC consulting while I was still employed at his agency.

One SBDC client was a woman from a nearby small town. Of all things—she was starting her own *advertising agency.* She had a background in insurance sales and was obviously a go-getter type. Her family was well established in a retail business, so she'd created newspaper ads and purchased local media. That was the extent of her advertising credentials.

I counseled her with some pointers on media and research techniques. She gave me pause … If she can make it … Maybe … Nope, too risky. My hard lessons of business failure were still deep scars etched into my hide after thirteen years of regular paychecks. *No way.*

Then, I interviewed with two other local agency owners. I believe one was only trying to get inside information about Mr. Cooper's agency. The other, Mr.

Jim Mudd wanted to offer me a position with his agency. However, his specialty, display classified and radio advertising for auto dealers, was a non-starter for me.

I'd gotten quite used to what David Ogilvy refers to as the "Intellectual Hothouse" atmosphere of a full-service ad agency. I was spoiled; I never got bored with my broad cross-section of clients. I still learn from all of them and their hybrid of industries every day. There's no age limit on self-renewal ... Or golf.

If Lady Beverly was Ms. Vitality, I was Mr. Variety.

7. A Few Moment-of-Truth Questions

As Mother's Day rolled around without me accepting a job offer. Gingerly, we began to think aloud of trying to make it on our own: Could we grow our own business?

Money?

Cash equals time, and time equals options. Cash equals time to find better clients. Just as my counter-offer to Mr. Cooper gave me time to sort out our options, a quick cash flow could make the difference between long-term success or failure.

After raising our five children, and Beverly resigning her full-time position, our cash reserves were still puny. But, there could be the almost-sure cash flow from the SBDC counseling; Uncle Sam pays his bills on time. Although, Mr. Pelham couldn't "guarantee anything."

On the plus side, we had minimal expenses and no debt. We drove two paid-for older Hondas, and lived frugally in that big old two-story duplex after all our children had moved on with their lives. Our expenses were down so low, even the goats could get at them.

Health insurance? We'd already bought our own, when Beverly left broadcasting and the agency didn't offer it. We were wizened veterans from almost getting screwed by the "Golden Finger" Insurance Company on a claim for Beverly's treatment as the result of a back injury.

Would any of my present agency clients come away with me? Who knows?

Mr. Cooper told me that when he started his own agency, he never told his clients when he left his previous shop, Colle-McVoy, until the following Monday. He "kept ten out of ten," he said.

Why do some new agencies fail?

They're impatient, nonprosperous and unfocused.

Why do some new agencies succeed?

They're patient and cautious, they think long-term; the rates they charge are high enough to give them a profit margin among the leaders. They specialize; they serve the leaders in their respective business categories, the old-established folks who pay their bills.

Where could we set up an office?

It's the duplex, stupid. But, with my belt-and-suspenders mind, I figured if we rented out the upstairs as an apartment, it would bring in more cash while we were getting up to speed.

We could live downstairs—almost free—and work in the huge, high-ceilinged living room with its sliding doors to close off the living space during the day.

Zoning? No problem; we were multi-family or professional offices.

What would we call the agency?

McCusker & Associates? Nope, sounds like a one-man band. Beverly would be working with me as we were getting started. How about ...

McCusker & McCusker?

Yes, that was it. *Sounds like* a father and son, or two brothers; an old reliable firm, good people who can be trusted, "yes, their money is good."

The name would be a bonus with all the women in our business sphere, who would be aware that the woman in the agency was an equal partner, at the time of the emerging Equal Rights Amendment. You go girl!

8. Hold Your Breath and Open the Doors

Monday, May 20, 1985 was the first day in business for the McCusker & McCusker advertising agency.

It was a stealth opening. We didn't put out any news releases. We wanted feedback from the market before a formal announcement ... in case (gulp) we failed.

I parked on our living room sofa and began calling previous clients. They all said they'd be happy to listen to our proposal. Ultimately, we only kept eight out of ten. Lucky for us, one of those two No's went bankrupt, then into the Federal Slammer for fraud.

I was amazed. I had no office, no stationery, no logo, no business phone, no computer; only my trusty yellow number two Ticonderoga pencils, and Beverly.

But, we had clients. I'd Identified Our Customers: The mother principle of entrepreneurship.

That afternoon, I met a SBDC client at a Perkins restaurant. Ms. Vickie Feldpouch was opening the Travel Store travel agency. I helped her with logo and ads. Her business has been a wonderful success over these intervening years. Ms. Vickie brought us First Day good luck.

By Father's Day on June 16th, after four weeks in business, we'd signed up four monthly retainer clients to almost equal my salary at the agency. Plus, we'd been assigned *fourteen* SBDC clients with payment to come from Uncle Sam.

We had promises for business from a total of twenty-one clients with projected annual income about 50-percent higher than my agency salary.

When our second-story tenant moved out after only two months, our dreams of slumlord wealth ended. So, we moved our little agency upstairs into 980 square feet of Victorian ambiance: all deductible.

The "World's Worst Advertising Agency" had found its "temporary" home for the next thirteen happy, prosperous years ... *two of the lucky 3-percent of Americans working in their residence.*

Later that summer, in a fit of extravagance, I finally invested fifty bucks in a bronze-looking, lawyerly-like, 13 X 14" shingle sign, which I mounted—with double sided tape—beside our front entrance door.

Then, the *Waterloo Cedar Falls Courier* gave us a wonderful above-the-fold news story on the Sunday Business Section cover.

By our first anniversary in 1986 we'd served a total of thirty-eight clients: twenty-nine came through the SBDC. Some of those had become full-service clients after their twenty hours of free time expired.

Our Social Capital account turned out to be our greatest asset. Years of community involvement and visibility had paid dividends beyond our greatest expectations. And apparently, there's always room for the little guy if you offer good service.

We were profitable almost from Day One. A business of your own can be profitable, if you bring in more money than you spend. *So, don't you forget those last three words.*

Finally, regarding the launch of our own business, we were able to do it ethically, while maintaining our respectful relationship with Mr. Cooper. I enjoyed my opportunity to work and learn with Frank. In my opinion, he was a great role model for a true agency professional. He's retired now.

9. Avoid Clients From Hell

HER COMPANY'S NAME was on the first check made out to McCusker & McCusker for $380, all ours, with no deductions. However, Uncle Sam gets his later.

She signed our first "written understanding," with the usual 60-day notice for termination of retainer by either party. We created a brochure for her. However, she never stopped complaining and changing every detail of our work.

I actually told her, "Why keep a dog and bark yourself?" She didn't take that meat-axe hint. She not only liked to bark, she thought she could chew on me.

Beverly swallowed hard when I told her I was going to resign our very first retainer account, *"For medical reasons … I'm sick of her."*

"Well, be nice and tell her we just don't think she'll ever be happy with our work," Bev said, sweetly.

The client's eyes popped open in disbelief when I resigned. It was our shortest retainer agreement ever.

Remember? I told you that cash equals options. We had a good enough handle on our cash flow right off the bat, so we could look for better clients.

Yes, you need customers … But not any one particular customer. That's what working for yourself is all about.

10. Use Alliances to Avoid Payroll

LUNKERS, as really big prize-winning bass are called, take years to put on their weight, as long as fifteen years.

Danilo Damjanovic (DAM-yon-o-vic) is one hellava graphic designer-illustrator, and a lunker of a hunter-fisherman. After working with Danilo for over twenty years, that fairly well sums it up for his talent and avocations.

Recently, he's marketing a series of prints depicting his paintings of the favorite catches for American Anglers. He's traveled all over the North American continent hunting bear, deer, caribou, wild boar, turkey and other critters—*with bow-and-arrow.*

Mr. Damjanovic was referred to our agency during our first full month of operation, by Dr. Paul Winters of the SBDC at UNI. He'd recently gotten his kick-in-the-pants (pink-slipped) by a woman who operated an agency in Waverly, a nearby small community. A lucky coincidence for us.

His introductory brochure demonstrated his sense of design, color, and his talent for illustration; as well as a certain shyness about his prosperous, farmer parent's Polish-Serbian immigrant name.

Danilo had named his free-lance art studio "Dan Draws." He was concerned about folks being able to pronounce his last name.

"Danilo, my friend, the world has learned how to pronounce Picasso, and Renoir," I said, "We'll just have to jam your last name down their throats."

Danilo immediately put his last name all alone at the top of all his communications. His well-established client list of blue-chip accounts has promptly paid his invoices ever since.

Mr. Damjanovic graduated from the Columbus College of Art & Design in 1977, after serving in the US Army. After learning with an architectural firm and several agencies, he began building his own business.

Danilo is a rare talent. He's comfortable illustrating cut-a-way views of boilers or exquisite executive pencil portraits. He's prompt, thorough, easy to work with, and perhaps best of all, he's no prima donna.

He's produced all of our agency's artwork since the beginning, as well as illustrating my other books.

He's prospered. I know he works harder than I do, but of course, he's fifteen years younger .

Danilo's visual imagery gives wings to my copywriter's roughs. We've proved many times over how we can do better things together, than each can do on our own. Advertising is a collaborative process.

11: Position Your Business, Then Hold to It

POSITIONING YOUR COMPANY or your product is critical to your success in getting a share of the customer's mind.

This marketing term was popularized in the Al Ries and Jack Trout book, *Positioning: the Battle for Your Mind,* published in 1981. They discuss Pepsi, Coke and the positioning of 7-Up as the Uncola. And Avis as "Number Two, but we try harder."

David Ogilvy defines the term as, "What the product does, and whom it is for." He positioned the Dove soap as a toilet bar for women, rather than detergent bar for men with dirty hands.

I alluded to this concept earlier in this book when we talked about finding your niche.

So, positioning or niche is *about* the same thing. For example, I positioned this book as a "Guide for Entrepreneurs." I could have positioned it as memoir autobiography for mainstream readers, but chose to sharpen my focus on *you* Dear Reader.

This discipline requires you to think through your target market/audience before spending one penny for marketing.

Once we knew our agency was going to survive, we positioned ourselves as a Business-to-Business & Agribusiness agency. By giving up lots of potential client categories—financials, autos, politicals—we gained more credibility in our chosen market.

Eventually, I was feeling frisky enough to create Memo notes for our own informal communications printed on one side as follows:

World's Worst Ad Agency

McCusker & McCusker is the world's worst advertising agency: no politicals, hamburgers, cola wars; no savings & loans, auto dealers, booze or butts; very little client turnover.

No vice presidents, department chiefs, review committees; no MBO, MBA's, or CPA's; no new cars, stock options, golden parachutes; no office politics, employee-of-the-month, back-stabbing; very little a__kissing.

No salaries—no sell, no eat—no debt; no laptops, modems, floppies—*no computer;* no WATTS line, bylaws, in-laws; no MTV, rock & roll, Muzak—no elevator; no smoking, wine-tasting, mind-bending drugs; very little hanky-panky.

Only Biz-to-Biz & Agribiz advertising; stop-you-in-your-tracks ideas; ads, brochures, videos; black belt in Direct Mail/Response; Bob's the creative, Bev watches the money, Dan draws; is this a great country or what?

-Copyright 1992 R. F. McCusker

This light-hearted positioning statement endeared us to our loyal clients and friends. Remember: Release and relax, lighten up, eat more ice cream.

12. Finding Your Niche, Cont'd

HERE'S A POTENTIAL niche product for you. We have been too busy to exploit this idea ourselves. Over the past thirty years there's been a growing need for a new type of dress. Here's a fast growing market, which can make you rich beyond avarice:

Maternity dresses, for high school girls ... In their appropriate school colors. Shhhhh ... Don't let anybody beat you to market.

13. Beware Blarney & Baloney

BLARNEY IS FLATTERY laid on just thin enough that you like it. e.g. "Thanks for giving your talk to my Kiwanis Club last month; you did a fine job <u>and</u> I truly enjoyed your book."

Baloney is flattery laid on so thick you choke on it.

A magazine writer was trying to flatter Jack Nicklaus in order to gain a valuable interview for a feature story.

"You're a fabulous golfer Mr. Nicklaus, you really know your way around the course; what's your secret" the writer asked.

"The holes are numbered," Jack deadpanned.

VI: HOW TO STAY FREE

Mr. Robert Ringer called it "Performance Power." You could have a ton of cash, all the legal agreements known to lawyers and still fail in your business. There is absolutely no better way to stay in business than to deliver the goods as promised. These marketing projects delivered.

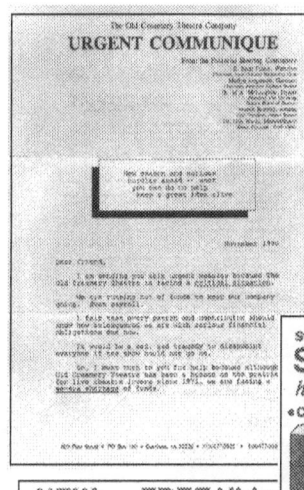

This simple black and white four-page appeal letter pulled in over $40,000 to keep the Old Creamery Theater going in a rustic Iowa town.

Below: B & W postcard pulled a record 1,300 inquires. Sadly, the product failed due to competition.
Advertising is not everything.

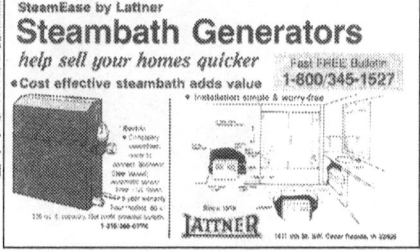

Left: This steady direct mail program reversed a five-year decline in enrollment for an Iowa Community College. McCusker then resigned the account when a committee of ladies was appointed to 'help' him.

With proliferation of media today, it behooves you to consider direct mail even for image advertising, rather than the usual response-rate goals. Here are two projects, which helped clients 'change' their image.

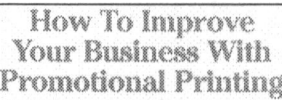

How To Improve Your Business With Promotional Printing
7-Minutes: A Comprehensive Approach to Maximizing Impact at Affordable Prices

A 125-year old forms printer acquired an established color printer, so they mailed thousands of these videos to tell the news.

※ 1-2-3-4 Color brochures, newsletters, stationery, catalogs, forms, posters, direct mail

MATT PARROTT
GOODFELLOW

514 Brattuber • PO Box 660 • Waterloo, IA 50704
1-800-728-4621 • 1-319-234-4621 • FAX 319-234-6199

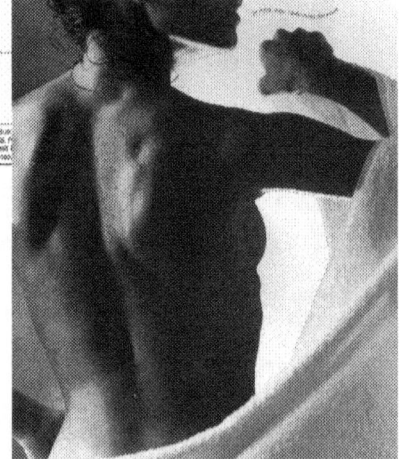

This steambath model's image was shown in three 'blind' teaser mailings, which preceded a large color poster for a new steam boiler product. The 700 list names were 699 male, one female. The one tiny line of copy from the model's lips says, "In a few days, I take away the towel." One can assume the recipients were looking for the next plain-brown envelope. [The one female wrote to the client asking, "Where's my hunk?"]

Ever heard of Krispy Kreme Doughnuts? Would you believe they don't advertise? They rely on free publicity generated by a concerted public service, community support image program. Here are long-running McCusker PR programs, which are continuing to yield the 'halo-effect.'

This PR Awards program is over ten years old and running strong. Given the 21st century CEO crime wave, there appears to be plenty of ethics and integrity scandal work to be done.

In 1986, just after the McCuskers launched their agency, they produced this public service campaign to 'unify and identify' their hometown area. At that time, eight area businesses included 'Cedar Valley' in their name. By 2004, over 75 organizations had adopted this name-identity.

Another community support project, which yielded exceptional PR value, is this local history co-authored by McCusker with client Mr. Dave Buck. A popular radio talk-show personality read one chapter per day for 30 days, plus promoted a book-signing event at the non-profit city museum.

The Waterloo newspaper featured their book in a 21-inch full column story. This sort of free publicity should continue for years.

"Between the gleam in Johann Gutenberg's eye when he invented moveable type in 1452, and the click of Tim Berners-Lee's mouse as in invented the World Wide Web in 1989, lies the first major revolution in the development of communications."

Gutenberg's type created a class of powerful, wealthy technical craftsmen. They eventually gave way to those in publishing who could create the 'content' for the new, cheaper books. Tim Berners-Lee, right, chose to remain in the background of the second communications revolution, which he created, rather than cash in on the dot.com boom.

After seven years online, this small-town client company has over 25,000 visitors every week to their website, which became the hub for the collision repair market of 65,000 bodyshops nationwide.

Advertising can help build a reputation for quality and service.
An advertiser's first challenge is credibility. Testimonials from experts work wonders
in Business-to-Business trade publications

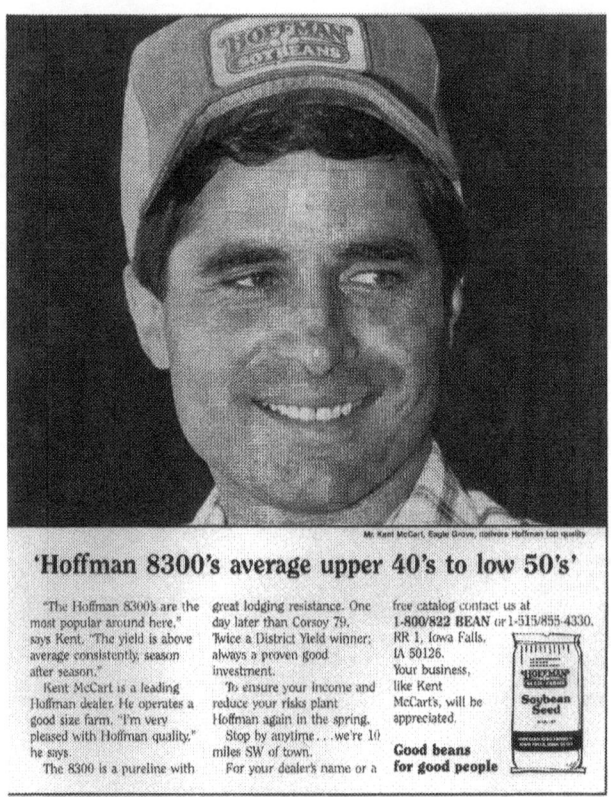

'Hoffman 8300's average upper 40's to low 50's'

"The Hoffman 8300's are the most popular around here," says Kent. "The yield is above average consistently, season after season."

Kent McCart is a leading Hoffman dealer. He operates a good size farm. "I'm very pleased with Hoffman quality," he says.

The 8300 is a pureline with great lodging resistance. One day later than Corsoy 79. Twice a District Yield winner; always a proven good investment.

To ensure your income and reduce your risks plant Hoffman again in the spring.

Stop by anytime . . . we're 10 miles SW of town.

For your dealer's name or a free catalog contact us at 1-800/822 BEAN or 1-515/855-4330. RR 1, Iowa Falls, IA 50126.

Your business, like Kent McCart's, will be appreciated.

Good beans for good people

Mr. Gary Hoffman approved this clean and simple design for his seed campaign, which ran for *thirteen years*, with five or six new testimonials each year. Most advertisers get sick of looking at the same images all the time, then ask for something 'new.' So, they don't achieve the Concentration X Repetition = Effectiveness of an 'Old Lonely,' the serviceman for Maytag, or 'Mr. Goodwrench' for General Motors.

14. Recognize the Power of Public Relations

HOW DO YOU POSITION A METRO AREA? How do you unify and identify a region the size of Connecticut?

An area 100 miles long by 50 miles wide: 5,000 square miles with high unemployment, low farm land prices, and a shortage of moving trailers because so
many were packing their bags.

Oh, by the way, do it without any money.

In 1986 we were into our second year of business. We were confident of our
survival. However, all around us, folks were having hard times. The John Deere
tractor operations went from 16,000 employees down to 6,000. The Rath
Packing Company pulled the plug in 1985; operations ceased after ninety-four
years. Thousands lost their job. Spirits sank in the metro and surrounding rural
area. The poor Federal Bankruptcy Judge was working himself to death.

This wasn't like some account executive/copywriter getting a kick in the pants.
This was big, and it was long-term.

Nevertheless, I *recognized a rich opportunity* for our fledgling agency to establish a reputation for good public service and public relations. If we could create
a sense of shared destiny for the 200,000 people within this region, the benefits
to us would be incalculable.

It may be Napoleonic, but in my gut, I've always believed one person can
make a difference.

And so, I started drafting with my yellow pencils, legal pads, and no money. I
knew where I wanted to get to—and that's usually half the battle.

The heart of the area is Waterloo, Cedar Falls, Evansdale and the rest of Black
Hawk County, Iowa.

Total population 130,000. Parts of surrounding counties added another
70,000 people.

There is only one element that connects everything: The Cedar River runs
right through the middle.

The word "Community" is pregnant with emotional possibilities, so it became
the keystone.

Our *Cedar Valley Communities* christening campaign was hatched in April of
1986. I invited the three cities' Chambers of Commerce officials to meet at our
office for—incredibly—their first-ever get together. They all said they'd support
our concepts.

That's when I discovered that in times of uncertain economic crisis, nobody is really in charge. There's plenty of finger pointing and bitching, but I couldn't identify an entity—political or otherwise—to "approve" our ideas.

Finally, I said, "Self, you're in charge. Lead the way, we'll be our own client for a free public service campaign."

Danilo began working on the graphic design logos to create the visual imagery we needed. I kept those old pencils smokin' to come up with this following essay:

About the Cedar Valley
Communities of Northeast Iowa

In the middle of the last century when settlers came to this river valley, there were no city limits.

Freedom was bounded only by the necessity of relying on each other; as in a family.

Big Brother looked after little sister, everyone knew everyone, and cared about each other.

By the middle of this century, easy economic times gave freedom to do one's own thing. Affluence was for everyone, bigger was better, so grow, and grow we did.

As the communities grew, neighbors became strangers. Big Brother began to mean something else.

Finally, the economy faltered. More talk, more studies, and more government entitlements failed to turn things around. Hard times came to the big company, the small business, the farmer, the family.

Now we remember why big brother must help lift the load. How good neighbors will see us through, and why the communities must pull together.

Attitudes are changing; but maybe it is a long-term achievement.

By the close of this century, history will prove the wisdom of working for the common good of the entire Cedar Valley. Future generations will have the opportunity to live, learn, and work in these beautiful communities with pride and optimism.

So forget not the Good Old Days; but now it's time to recall our Spirit of One Community.

—R.F. McCusker, 4 July 1986

THIS PROSE essay was printed on elegant stock by our client Matt Parrott & Sons and widely distributed to the centers-of-influence folks.

The local media came through with Public Service Announcements (PSA's) time and space to carry the message and our logo. A $10,000 rotary billboard was donated by the media and moved around our area over the next year. The Courier was a big editorial booster for the message. All of the influential leaders were in support. *Concentration x Repetition = Effectiveness* was tested on a grand scale.

Did it work?

When we kicked off the campaign in 1986, there were eight companies listed in the city directory with the words "Cedar Valley" in their name.

By 2004's Cedar Valley Area phone directory, there are over seventy-five businesses and organizations named the Cedar Valley something-or-other.

Even the biggest church in the metro area had changed their name from Sunnyside Temple to Cedar Valley Community Church.

Every day, almost every one of our 200,000 residents may use the phrase "Cedar Valley" in their daily lives.

Those city-limit-sign barriers in the minds of the residents dissolved fairly quickly once there was something better positioned for their vision of where they lived.

It's succeeded beyond our wildest hopes and dreams. Plus, our local widely diversified Cedar Valley economy is in great shape again.

Sure, I was the right guy in the right place at the right time. However, I had the anatomy of a burglar, and the faithful support of Beverly and Danilo to see us through.

We'd risked a lot of billable hours before we knew if our work would ever see the light of day.

For the record, we never received any money from anyone for the use of our copyrighted intellectual property. We weren't expecting any money. We were a new business looking to gain the "halo effect" for our contributions. BINGO! We achieved our goal and then some.

Fourteen years later, in 1999, the Courier did another feature story with color photos, to recognize our agency and our creation of the campaign.

Then, I leveraged that visibility into *another project* with three more Business section cover stories: The *Cedar Valley Entrepreneurs of the Century Calendar: 1900–2000*. I selected them, did the research and writing; Danilo did fourteen terrific illustrations. We earned our expenses and $3,000 for UNI scholarships.

Finally, in 2003, I co-authored *Meeting Your Waterloo* with client Dave Buck, a local history to commemorate out hometown's sesquicentennial. Our image of community support has deep roots and a firm foundation. And it continues to pay dividends.

It's a fact: One dollar spent on Public Relations may do the job of ten spent on advertising, and it's more credible. Include the Power of PR in your spending plans for communications.

Or, if you're really lucky like us, you'll get tens of thousands of dollars of free visibility for your ideas. I must confess though, this was one from the heart, as well as for the wallet.

15. Entrepreneurs Can Make a Come Back

IN 1978 HOWARD JARVIS led a taxpayer's revolt in California which passed Proposition 13 to slash property taxes by 57 percent. Every politician in America wanted his or her picture taken with Mr. Jarvis, including Jimmy Carter, for the cover of *TIME*.

Jarvis' rise from obscurity at age seventy-five prompted him to say, "The sweetest sugar is all at the bottom of the cup." I loved the quote and filed it in my memory bank.

Twelve years later, when I started writing poetry, I had the same feelings about our minor, Phoenix-like success as an agency. Mr. Jarvis died in 1986, so I didn't think he'd mind if I liberated his line.

This verse has been helpful to several friends when their spirits were low:

THE SWEETEST SUGAR

~For Annie

At some point in our lives, we may find ourselves
down on our luck, even in this great country
of ours; with the opportunity to succeed
comes the chance for failure. Mistakes are made,
we over-reach for the brass ring, accidents
happen, good health leaves us, marriages fail;
our hopes are dashed.

When our predicament dawns on us—slowly
as first—we realize things will never be the
same as they were, and hard times may be here
for many long, long years; our hopes grow dim.

"We must take the long view,"
said Brubeck the composer.
"Do not be discouraged by
setbacks, they are inevitable
but rather remember, life
runs in cycles like a wheel,
sometimes we are on the spoke

facing down, but with
perseverance, everything
comes around, and we are soon
turning toward the top again."

New generations live longer now, we have more
years to succeed, then perchance to fail, yet
recover again. Hope teaches us to hold fast to
our spoke, then discover in our later years,
the sweetest sugar of all, is at the bottom
of the cup, and hope will conquer our fears.

I did research on legendary baseball pitcher Leroy "Satchel" Paige for Danilo to illustrate beside the verse. His arm had given out in the middle of his career; he thought he'd never pitch again.

But he did come back ... to pitch for a total of forty-three years. This was his record:

He pitched over 2,500 games; he won about 2,000 of them. He pitched over 300 shutouts, and fifty-five, yes, *fifty-five no-hitters*. Several times he had twenty-two strikeouts per game. He played summer and winter, once pitching 153 games in a single season.

16. McCusker's Law

MCCUSKER'S LAW states that Murphy's Law is too optimistic.

17. Sure-Fire Recipe for Writing an Advertisement

HERE'S A RECIPE for writing an ad that always works. I use the word "ad" for any type of communication. It works for radio, television, book titles (like this one), direct mail and news releases.

1. *Headline 2. Subhead 3. Bullets 4. Text 5. Action Call.*

Here's a sample trade journal ad following this recipe:

(include a photo or cut-away illustration of the product in your layout)

1) Headline: NEW—LATTNER BOILERS

2) Subhead: Four-Pass Efficiency for More Steam, Less Energy

3) Bullets: * 5 Sizes, Steam 10–30 HP Front & Center Power Burner

                 * Total Package Units, Ready to Connect

                 * Water Feed Systems, Condensate Tanks

4) Text Copy: (words to fit space/time to help create Desire phase).

5) Action Call: FREE VIDEO/BULLETINS
                 800 Telephone Number
                 Nitty Gritty: Fax, E-mail, address etc.

If you follow this recipe and remember the fundamental AIDA: Attention, Interest, Desire, Action, you will produce credible communications with practice.

A century ago, the best words to use in headlines were: New, Free, You and Your. *They're still the best.*

Be sure to include lots of WIIFM's in your copywriting: What's In It For Me? That's why the prospect is paying attention to your message.

18. 'Do What You Do Best and Hire the Rest.'

MR. GARY HOFFMAN, owner and CEO of Hoffman Seed Farms, may not have known it, but he was quoting the English economist, David Recardo, when he told me of his philosophy: "*Do what you do best and hire the rest.*"

Recardo (1772–1823) advanced his "Theory of Comparative Value" for trading among nations. "Stick to your specialty" was his message.

For example, if you're a consultant earning $100 per hour, you should hire a secretary to do your typing at $20 per hour, rather than burn your candle at both ends trying to do everything. Conserve your energy.

It's great advice for any small businessperson that desires to be a big businessperson.

Mr. Hoffman first told me that little saying in 1982 when he hired Mr. Cooper's agency to expand his market for soybean seed sales in Central Iowa.

Gary loves the production side of farming, but wasn't too keen on some of the backslapping required for building a network of dealers and sales agents. He'd hired Mr. Tom Blome as his sales manager, and then I got involved for the agency.

Together, over the next thirteen years, we'd build Hoffman's business reputation and image as a quality seed supplier. Mr. Hoffman then sold out to a major seed company. Gary stayed active on the production side and left the marketing to others.

Thirteen years doesn't seem so long when you just read the words. However, Tom Blome's little boy started Kindergarten the year I started on the account.

Tom's now full-grown son graduated from high school the year we finished our work for Mr. Hoffman.

We developed a long-term, farmer testimonial campaign with the tagline, "Good Beans … for Good People." We ran targeted B & W print ads in the agribusiness papers, which we could buy on a county-by-county basis.

Then we backed up the newspaper ads with Outdoor billboards in selected target areas with the local dealer's "snipe" banner across the bottom.

Hoffman's seed catalogs and direct mail echoed the theme. We added limited flights of statewide radio and an uncommon publics relations program: signed and numbered, Art Prints.

We commissioned an original series of three barn painting prints, sending them to key farmer "centers-of-influence," which we carefully identified.

The prints were delivered via UPS to winners in the statewide yield contests, and media types. Imagine what a fine impression Hoffman Seed made when those brown trucks rolled into the farmstead bearing a—totally unexpected—valuable gift.

Mr. Hoffman's family-based farm business reflected his wholesome outlook on life. Gary's daughter, Teresa, quoted Gary: "If you can adapt, you'll always be happy," and he seems like a very happy man.

19. On Avoiding Trouble With Money

OTHER PEOPLE'S MONEY AND BAD DEBTS are trouble spots we avoided by carefully selecting our clientele. (Of course, you'll take care of your taxes too).

Earlier, I hypothesized why some new agencies succeed: They specialize; they serve the leaders in their respective business categories, the old-established folks who pay their bills.

About Other People's Money:
1) I'd known some fast–talking agency types who thought they could live on "The Float:" cash from their clients, which was due to the media in short order.
2) They acted like that thousand dollars—from a media buy—was theirs, when only 15 percent, $150, was their *gross profit.* If they were really

clever, their *net profit* would be 20 percent of that: $30. If you're extending media credit to advertising clients, you're risking a $1,000 loss against $30. The odds are better in Las Vegas.

3) We considered client's money as "No Touchies," another Robert Ringer tip. We prefer to work on a professional service fee basis, plus mark-up on purchases, and then pass the commissions directly on to the client by having the media bill the client directly at their net rate. No Touchy, No Temptation, or false sense of wealth.

About Bad Debts:

Our beginning strategy was to work with the old, established companies. After several years, I scanned our client list. Amongst the red glass were these rubies: (By year established)

1856	A. Y. McDonald
1868	Matt Parrott & Sons
1890	Grundy Light & Power
1890	Ellsworth College
1892	Henkel Construction
1900	Clay Equipment
1918	Lattner Boiler
1932	Hoffman Seed

We've collected 99.997% of the money we earned. We went to small claims court twice: one win, one loss. (The SOB lied under oath).

Seller Beware: even this strategy is not perfect. Our poor friends at employee-owned Clay Equipment recently went into bankruptcy after 100 years.

Finally on this topic, what's the value of your Accounts Receivable Dollar? *

30 Days past due		.97
90	"	.90
120	"	.80
180	"	.67
1 Year	"	.40
2 Years	"	.23
3 Years	"	.12

*U.S. Dept. Commerce

20. ABC's of Market Research for Ellsworth College

IN 1994 WE WERE BROUGHT IN to stem the tide of falling enrollment. Mr. Gary Hoffman, Hoffman Seed, arranged for us to address the board of trustees, which was vitally interested in a swift turnaround after many years of revenue decline.

Mr. Hoffman, a long-time board member, introduced us to the board in a manner, which demonstrated his confidence in our agency to help restore the flow of cash at an average of $4,000 per student per year.

This prosperous century-old Community College has deep roots and a firm foundation in Iowa Falls, Iowa, an American-Gothic town of four thousand. It began as a religious institution, then became part of the Iowa state system with enrollment at 700–800 students.

A switch in state law was responsible for the decline. Suddenly, the purely technical community colleges around the state could start offering the Liberal Arts junior college courses, which were the bread-and-butter for Ellsworth.

Rather than moving into Iowa Falls, fifty miles from Waterloo or Des Moines, young Suzy or Johnny could live at home and attend the previously all technical colleges in their own community.

Competition had reared its ugly head in Pleasantville. Dormitories were quieter, classes were leaner ... it was time to put some more bottoms on the desk chairs.

The faculty and administrative staff had tried all the usual tactics: a student opinion survey, their catalogs extolling the beautiful campus, some radio and newspaper ads plus direct mail to high school seniors. Still, enrollment headed south.

Beverly and I put on our best duds to appear before this wonderful group of fourteen volunteers trying to find the right path for their greatest local asset. After Gary's introduction and a quick review of our credentials, which included nothing about marketing Education, I presented my proposal.

"I don't know what the answers are," I said, "but I know what the questions are.

One, W*hen* do students start thinking about college choice?

Two, *What* are the choice factors?"

I went to explain that without the answers to those critical questions, they'd be shooting in the dark, at the wrong time.

The board members warmed to the ideas. One asked what we'd need to get started and what kind of a budget would make a dent in the problem.

I shot from the hip and offered to do a preliminary marketing analysis, recommendations and options report for $1,800. I ballpark-estimated that the income from ten additional students, $40,000, could turn things around if invested c-a-r-e-f-u-l-l-y.

I'd *recognized another rich opportunity.* I was risking some of our billable agency hours to find a solution and gain a long-term client.

When we arrived back at the office there was a message to call Mr. Hoffman. He said the board had voted unanimously to approve our preliminary report fee. "Get to work." Gary said.

Put yourself in my place. Where would you start?

"Primary" research—which you do yourself—is expensive and time consuming. Somebody else has already done "Secondary" research ... if you can find it.

I started calling editors of the trade publications aimed at the college recruiters, board members and trustees, to see if any studies had been done on our two key questions.

On the fourth call, an editor asked if I'd checked with Eric?

"Eric who?" I said.

"That's ERIC, the Education Research Institute for Community Colleges, located at UCLA," the editor said, "here's their phone number."

I gave him the Old Irish blessing, "May you be in Heaven an hour before the devil knows you're dead."

I called ERIC, talked with a chatty clerk, who looked into her computer screen to report, "Yes, there are about *twenty-five studies on those topics.*"

"Do you have access to the Internet?" she asked.

"What's that?" I said.

"It's a computer network for government and educational institutions. Here's what I can do. I'll print out this list and fax it to you. You pick out the ones you want ... then I'll print them out and mail them to you. You can use a credit card to pay for the reproduction fees," she said.

Within minutes the list came in. BINGO!

I selected ten research titles, then gave the lady my credit card number for a fee of *seventy-five dollars.*

In a few days we got our ten-inch stack of research on the questions crucial to our success:

One: 38% of students begin making college plans *before* their junior year and 44% during their junior year. Total: 82% were in the market long before Ellsworth made initial contact.

Two: If you teach it, they will come. Offering a major in the student's field is the first criterion. Also, cost and financial aid factors cluster at the top of the potential student's needs/interests scale.

From this cornucopia of data we also gleaned other key factors: Mass media was a waste of money; Counselors were the centers-of-influence; Smaller was better, safer and friendlier; the emotional side of the student shouldn't be ignored; The Visit to the campus was the final deciding element for the student/parent choice. All that for seventy-five bucks. Such a deal.

We presented our findings and proposals to the Board:

A. Position Ellsworth: Where 72% get financial aid; over 60 major fields of study.

B. Focus on high schools within 60–100 miles; especially developing relationships with the over–worked counselors.

C. Identify Ellsworth and Iowa Falls as one; smaller is better and safer for those tender young farm girls and boys.

D. We detailed some ballpark–estimates for creative and production costs for catalogs, direct mail, posters and a video to sell the Visit, not the college.

It was the anti slam-bang, big media budget. It was my favorite, pleasant orthodontia approach: the targeted, gradual pressure over the next few years to shape a clear-cut image.

The board hired us and away we went.

Did it work?

By the third year enrollment was up 15-percent; about 100 more students at $4,000 per bottom. The Direct Mail wheel kept on turning; videos went out, campus visits were up. Happiness returned to Pleasantville.

Mr. Philip Rusley, Admissions Director, and I got along famously. I wrote and produced the 7-minute video featuring a young girl and her mother visiting the campus.

We created posters with coupons for the FREE video to be hung near the counselor's office. (We borrowed that idea from the Army/Navy/USMC. The old is forever new). We mailed fine leather coffee-mug coasters to hundreds of counselors and handed them out at their trade-shows.

And, our agency was earning good money from the account.

Now, what could go wrong?

Then, the old Dean retired.

The new Dean came in with her own ideas of how things had worked in the bigger market she came from in the Southwest.

She invited me to a meeting with her "marketing committee". I looked around the table at six female faces: Neophytes and volunteer do-gooders. They "had some fresh ideas they wanted to share" with me. It was the committee from hell, for this old pro. CLASH.

"Ring the bell, school's out for me here," I said to myself. We were out of that class picture within months. Personalities mean a lot in our business.

Footnote: In the spring of 2001, our newspaper reported how the new Dean lost a faculty vote of confidence: 24–6. She decided to take early retirement. Clients come, clients go; in the end we only have each other.

21. The Five Ages of Man

AT THREE SCORE AND TEN, I noticed these to be true:
1) Youth 2) Middle Age 3) "You're looking good, Bob." 4) You forget to zip up 5) Finally, you forget to zip down.

22. The Simple Life Will Set You Free

"A DAMN CLOSE RUN THING," is how the Duke of Wellington described the Battle of Waterloo.

Since 1991, I've been in the battle of Waterloo at Gates Park Golf Course every Friday afternoon from St. Patrick's Day to Thanksgiving. And, it's always a damn close run thing. That's why it's so much fun.

Mr. Dean Diamond was the national sales manager for Paris & Sons when we first started our regular golf match on Fridays. Dean was responsible for establishing and directing a national network of independent sales agents and representatives.

We created Paris' packaging designs for their consumer Ice Melter and Lawn & Garden product lines. Then we added sales brochures and ad specialty items for extra promotion on new product launches.

Dean's easy to work with, has high energy and a very similar youth to mine. At eight years younger, he's tougher to beat on the links every year. However, we can play sixteen rounds and have a one-stroke difference, as we did one year. (Dean was ahead).

Mr. Leo Telepnev, now a retired mechanical contractor's chief estimator and (choke, a natural enemy) purchasing agent, was the third to become a regular. He's Dean's partner in the team matches and a fierce competitor.

Mr. Mark Niedert is my partner. Mark is a superb salesman and new business promoter. His advice: "Never talk business on the golf course before the fifth hole, and never after the fifteenth hole."

Mr. John Cessna, a computer programmer from Cedar Rapids, joins us sometimes as a fifth. This 6'2" long-driving machine is as lean as a two-iron. Once, on season opening day, he drove the 55-miles to play with us. Due to his rusty putting skills, we took him for a bunch of "crispies" (dollar bills). We all offered to send a cab for him the next week. Later, he got even with us.

I call it the *Friday Dog Fight* because it sounds like a pack of dogs, yapping and whining over the day's local rules, side bets, who's walking on whose putting line, handicaps and sore-back excuses. We play a two-dollar team Nassau, and halves for extra points in a flock of short-shot games.

It's always a matter of life-or-death competition, but when those mellow afternoons are over, there are no bodies.

Only memories of men being boys forever.

These gentlemen are also a great sounding board for business ideas: unvarnished opinions are valuable to the sometimes-isolated small businessperson.

I included this topic to demonstrate that "success" isn't only about adding more zeros to your bank balance.

Recreational sports have done more for mental health than all the doctors in the world have. Tension and stress can kill you. Let it out, live healthier and longer.

For Less Worry: *The simple life will set you free.*

23. Beware of Those Rocking Chair Taxes

ALERT FOR THE SOON-TO-BE SELF-EMPLOYED: Your FICA Social Security/Medicare tax is about to double. Your employer has been paying the same amount as you have. Now you'll pay over 15%. e.g. $100,000 income = $13,427, *plus income taxes.*

24. Three of Our Best Direct Mail Packages

THE OFFER AND THE LIST are the two most important elements for your planning stage in direct mail communications.

The Offer must be instantly visible at-a-glance. "Tell me quick and tell me true, or else my friend, to hell with you" is vitally important with the daily deluge of mail. e.g. Get a FREE Issue, SAVE $100 Rebate, 12 Bags @ $7.50/bag, FREE SAMPLE ENCLOSED, etc.

The more time and effort you invest to increase the effectiveness of your Offer, the greater your Return on Investment (ROI). Then, simplify your graphics so the offer leaps from the envelope or page to the eye.

The List of names your direct mail is mailed to is the second critical element for success. Success being defined as at least the national average of a 1-percent response rate. (Magazine subscription advertisers are happy with a seven-tenths of 1-percent response rate).

Your customer list of names is the greatest asset for direct mail. It's like fishing in the aquarium versus fishing in the ocean.

Your agency and printers maintain sources for all kinds of lists. This digital age allows us to slice and dice the lists for all kinds of demographic sorts.

The Federal SBA has classified all businesses into Standard Industrial Classification (SIC) Codes. So, you can select your target names from a list by SIC code, then the sub headings of ZIP codes, income, number of employees, etc.

Once you have your Offer and List nailed down, then you move on to how to put together your package with your AIDA guidelines. Every mailing allows you the opportunity to *test* something. Results are measurable: reply cards, coupons, checks and orders, telephone calls.

I'm only half-joking when I claim to have a Black Belt in direct mail. We've created many, many successful packages for our clients over the years.

Here are three of our best direct mail packages, in chronological order:

HOFFMAN SEED'S HOFFTEST PROGRAM

Farmers are just like you and me; they're prone to follow the creme de la creme, even when buying new varieties of seed stock. So, with Gary Hoffman's blessing, we created a long-term direct mail program, which focused upon the centers-of-influence top producers.

Rather than saying, "Here are some good beans cheap," I pulled the pseudo research "HOFFTEST PROGRAM" from the recesses of my copywriter's mind. We used our bread-and-butter 9 x 6" envelope, with seed guide/catalog, letter and BRM reply card.

The "pitch letter" copy went something like this:

"You are cordially invited to participate in our proprietary soybean seed on-farm evaluation program:

HOFFTEST '84. You may reserve 12-bags of proprietary seed at your special evaluation price of $7.50/bag. Nothing else to buy. Simply mail the enclosed reservation card on or by Feb. 15th. Supplies limited." The letter went on with the who, why, where and how research details. The PS at the end always repeats the offer, because many readers start there first out of sheer curiosity.

The offer was based upon the bargain appeal—about half price—and the farmer's desire to be in something new; get the latest information on moneymakers in his area. Most of the farmers had 12-row planters, so they could have enough seed for a tidy test strip.

Our strategy was to systematically seed—no pun intended—each county we expanded into with these top producers. Hopefully, their neighbor farmers would follow along and try some Hoffman Seed. They did.

We purchased our list of 5,000 names (minimum) from the *Farm Journal* magazine, sorted by county, number of acres farmed, type of crops, then pared that down to 2,000–2,500: deleting present customers, competitors, poor credit risks, etc.

On all four pieces in the package, the offer leaps to the eye: 12 Bags @ $7.50/bag. The package was mailed bulk rate third class—first class postage does not increase response rates.

Since we were after actual orders—not just requests for free information—I wasn't sure how we'd do. Our agribusiness newspaper campaign, and Hoffman's sterling reputation for quality and published ISU University yield test results helped pave the way when our package showed up in the farmer's mailbox.

That first mailing and every mailing for the *next ten years* produced an astounding 4 to 5-percent response for orders. Each year we picked up 150–250 new 'HOFFTEST' users. Most went on to be great heavy users and or dealers for the entire line of seed varieties. Hoffman's sales staff delivered the seed, and was able to establish warm, long-term relationships with the follow-up reports required for our "research program."

Repeat your winners, and kill your losers. You'll know in hurry, which is which with direct mail.

SAVING THE OLD CREAMERY THEATRE

TWO GENTLEMEN FROM WATEROO came to see us about helping them save the Old Creamery Theatre from going under in 1990.

The OCT was founded in the picturesque—dinky—rural town of Garrison, Iowa, between Cedar Rapids and Waterloo, in a charming old co-op dairy building. It operated from May to October with a full buffet dinner inside or a picnic basket in the Courtyard.

The twenty-year old non-profit playhouse featured professional actors performing high-quality theatre. They had always operated hand-to-mouth, however this time they were on life-support and barely breathing financially.

OCT board members, Mr. Gene Enderlein, retired clothier, and Mr. Rod Geist, successful insurance executive and actor par excellence, liked the tone of the copy in an ad we ran in the local symphony program for our own agency. Apparently, it *does* pay to advertise.

Could we create a fundraising letter for them?

Considering their plight, and Beverly's love of live theatre, I told them I'd do it for no fees, but if we could put money in their treasury, then we wanted our fair share. Literally, No Sell No Eat. We shook hands on the deal.

We had to convince those folks OCT had been begging from for twenty years, that this time it really was life-or-death. We had to do it fast, and do it cheap. They had a list of 20,000 names—lots of farm families—they had been pounding on with shrinking results, but it was a place to start.

This time I created a "Financial Steering Committee" with some of the biggest names in Northeast Iowa: a dominant bank chairman, the national chairman of the American Soybean Assoc., president of the OCT board of directors, the past president of the Amana Society, and a senior physician of the renowned Wolfe Clinic. They all approved the use of their names.

This list of marquee names on the outside of the plain-vanilla white #10 envelope from the OCT, and at the top of the letter inside lent our message *credibility.*

Our second challenge was to create a serious *sense of urgency.* I wrote a four-page, black ink on economy white paper, pitch letter under the headline in stark black type:

U R G E N T C O M M U N I Q U E

"New season and serious hurdles ahead—what you can do to help keep a great idea alive ... "

I went on to describe the "<u>critical situation, the severe shortage of funds, making cuts in staff salaries,</u> and how many others are working hard to <u>secure the future</u> of OCT." I outlined the Power of A Plan.

Then I described the exciting New Season ahead ... revived their memories of their last visit to the Theatre: "What Acting! ... Singing! ... Fun!"

Here's the P. S.:

"This is the <u>most critical situation</u> we've ever had. It is a rare philanthropic opportunity when a modest gift can make a major difference. Won't you please come to our aid by sending your gift right now ... <u>TODAY!</u> Thank you."

We included a self-addressed remittance envelope with gift size choices, addressed back to the Financial Steering Committee.

17,603 pieces were mailed the day after Thanksgiving as generous hearts were opening for the Holiday season.

The OCT hoped to collect $20,000 to tide them over the winter and then perhaps make a long-term arrangement with the nearby, world famous Amana Colonies.

The checks started to pour in: 215 in the first two weeks.

On December 3rd, a letter arrived from a major contributor's Foundation secretary.

"What a wonderful letter—it should strike a chord in the hearts of all who have been entertained over the years ... it is very refreshing to have a <u>communiqué</u> from someone who has the same concerns as I do."

She generously stated she was canceling, and forgiving as Paid in Full, $8,500 of the $10,000 she had loaned the OCT, "to alleviate most of the problem."

By the fifteenth of January the OCT had opened their mail to the tune of $31,500 plus the forgiven $8,500: Total $40,000. More checks trickled in later.

On with the SHOW!

I sent them an invoice for our services, which they cheerfully paid.

And we all lived happily ever afterward.

Curtain Down.

LATTNER BOILER'S PERCEIVED IMAGE

REMEMBER THE OLD STEAM LOCOMOTIVES belching smoke and blowing their steam whistles? That steam engine is basically a horizontal boiler; a very efficient design to achieve maximum HorsePower per square foot of heating surface.

The Lattner Boiler Co. has been building horizontal boilers since 1950. They've installed over 50,000 boilers of all types around the world since 1918. They've usually operated with 50–75 employees. (See lattner.com)

Mr. Steve Junge is CEO and owner of Lattner. We met in 1979 when I was prospecting for new clients, with the Letter-Telephone-Letter technique described in the Lifeblood of Business topic.

Steve was our agency's first full-service client to sign up when Beverly and I hung out our shingle. His support for us is deep and wide. We've tried to do our best for all of Lattner's wonderful staff, which includes my coordinators, Carol Hawkins and Marge Junge.

Mr. Junge is a thoroughbred athlete; he'd been a ski instructor in Aspen before returning to Cedar Rapids to lead their family-based business. In recent years, even as age fifty crept upon him, he qualified and rode in the quadrennial Paris-Brest-Paris bicycle race; a distance of 746 miles *nonstop*. He achieved his time goal without nodding off and crashing as some of the 3,500 riders do.

His wife, Tris, surprised him with a rare gift: a complete trip to the Himalayas with a Mount Everest team. Steve flew into Kathmandu, then climbed with the team to the Base Camp at 17,500 feet.

So, you can see, this is a man who takes a risk now and then.

Lattner's Horizontal Return Tubular (HRT) boiler is the Rolls Royce of boilers for the Laundry and DryCleaning (L&DC) market segment. It's perfect for dry steam to operate all the pressing equipment: lots of steam, and as dependable as my mother's old Maytag wringer washing machine.

Over half of Lattner's sales volume is in the L &DC market, with other industrial segments added for diversity.

Alas, competition reared its ugly head.

First: A New York boiler company gradually made inroads with a Vertical Tubeless type boiler. So many of the L&DC plants were moving into high priced mall real estate that space became a critical cost factor. Vertical Compactness was in, Horizontal HRT "Rolls Royces" were out.

Second: Korean immigrants took over 30-percent of the national L&DC markets; and 80–90-percent of some major metro markets. Few of them spoke fluent English. *How to communicate with them?*

We dealt with the Korean communication problem first, by translating Lattner's sales bulletins and video. We advertised in the Korean trade publications consistently.

Then we created a logo/symbol to appeal to the Koreans without offending our long-time American customers. The symbol was a stylized Ying Yang circle; similar to the one used in the center of the *South Korean flag*. The Koreans recognized it instantly and smiled broadly: Lattner *understood* how difficult it is to move into a foreign country and communicate.

We added the Ying Yang symbol to all the bulletins and product decals. Americans thought they saw a Pepsi-like water and steam symbol. No problem. Cool.

Mr. Junge's engineering team retooled some of their old-established designs and created a superior Vertical Tubeless to compete. Sales picked up to offset the long-term decline in HRT's.

By the mid 1990's, Steve and I concurred that while he had the vertical products, the L&DC market still perceived Latter as the "Old Reliable HRT People."

It takes about *five years* to really make a dent in the minds of the industrial markets with trade publication advertising. Double-page spreads would cost too much: About $9,000 for *American Drycleaner's* circulation of 22,000. Fractional page ads wouldn't have enough impact.

We knew from all our experience that Concentration and Repetition was the key to Effectiveness.

How about a direct mail campaign?

We could concentrate on the Centers of Influence in the marketplace: About 700 key people; an easy List to create. It turned out to be 699 men and *one woman.*

The worst response to the first trade ad I ever created for Lattner was *one* inquiry for $700. However, my best response for a direct mail postcard in a

Homebuilder's postcard deck was also for Lattner: 1,300 replies for a free brochure on a new residential steambath boiler Steve brought to market. We about swamped Ms. Carol Hawkins with those requests.

Steve quickly learned the residential market was too foreign to his industrial market base. He threw in the towel and moved on. Kill your losers quick.

Serendipity: We still had the luxurious black-and-white photos we shot for the residential steambath brochure. A beautiful female draped with a towel, covered with beads of perspiration after her Lattner boiler steambath—very sensual, but not sexist.

AIDA: Attention, Interest, Desire and Action.

How do you get the attention and interest of 699 men? How about creating some Sex Appeal, presented in a mysterious, though endearing, series of blind mailings? No client identity, return address, etc.

We selected a series of three photos from the steambath brochure. Then we added one, tiny wavy line of copy emerging from the model's lovely lips in *8-point Italics like this.*

We selected Julin Printing, which has a branch office in Dubuque, Iowa to do the near-museum-quality printing and mailing; that way Lattner's hometown of Cedar Rapids wouldn't be evident on the plain brown 13 x 10" envelopes, or the final mailing tube containing a full-color *poster.*

The mailings went out one per week over a four-week span.

Mailing # 1: Head and shoulders photo of the lovely, water-beaded model holding a towel up to her bosom near the bottom of the image. From her lips, one line: "In a few days ... I lower the towel." Hmmm.

Mailing # 2: Backside view of the same model, cropped from her head's profile at the lips, down to her sacroiliac; she's lowered the towel well away from her Venus-like figure. Her lips whispered: "In a few days ... I take away the towel." Hmmmmm.

Mailing #3: Close-up of a curvaceous portion of the same model's thigh or shoulder—one cannot tell for certain—with rivulets of perspiration or beads of water poised for that lucky towel off to the side of the image. Her lips: "In a few days ... I will show you something very, very, very steamy." Hmmmmmmmm!

Mailing #4: A mailing tube containing a gorgeous 24 x 33" four-color poster revealing a full-length frontal view of ... Lattner's Vertical Tubeless boiler. (*Curses!*) She's topless, has a smooth, mirror-like outer skin of Stainless Steel, and hung with knobs and gauges to excite the Boilermen of the World.

The FAB's—features, advantages, and benefits—are listed as the "Top ten reasons to invest in Lattner." The poster had a super secondary use as a sales-training tool for the dealer's sales force.

Our water-beaded Venus model—with lucky towel—appears on the reply-card with her usual one line of copy: "Here's something very, very, very steamy." The brief copy offered up-to-date bulletins and video.

699 hearts were broken, but 1,398 eyes were opened to the fact that Lattner was a Player in the Vertical boiler market.

The 700 th pair of eyes belonged to the only woman—a Korean lady in Washington, DC—on our list. She sent Mr. Junge a letter of complaint.

"When was he going to do a mailing which featured some 'real hunks' for her?" HAR!

Steve received all kinds of replies, phone calls and faxes about the series. He told me it was the best thing we ever did for him; at a fraction of the cost for one spread in a national trade publication.

So, there you have it.

Exceeded only by the rare personal sales letter, direct mail can be a powerful partner in marketing. Following my fundamental guidelines will enhance your odds of success.

When our present clients read this section, perhaps they'll think, well, maybe he does have a good idea once in a while; looks like about like one every five years at this rate.

25. Avoid Allergies Anonymous

MR. STEVE MARAVETZ has been a great friend and accomplice to many of the literary crimes I've committed over the past twenty years. As a magazine editor he published my verses and business articles.

The value of his encouragement with this book is incalculable.

These days, Steve is in PR as Director of Health Science Relations at the University of Iowa, and *still* a sorry golfer by his own latest confession.

When he was married to Ms. Dixie Collins, at one of the most beautiful outdoor weddings in Palisades-Kepler State Park, I gladly attended to share in his joy.

During the gala reception afterward he noticed my diet cola in hand, then asked why I never drank alcohol.

"Stever, old friend, I'm allergic to alcohol," I said. "It makes me break out. Break out windows … break out teeth … "

Years later, Steve said, "I quit too; add me into the 10-percent of our population that are also allergic."

Be careful with that stuff, it can set you back years.

26. Choose Integrity & Leadership

T. WAYNE DAVIS and Marvin Klepfer, were my mentors during the formative years of my career. They were examples of how to operate a business based upon integrity and fair play.

Over the years, when I thought of T. Wayne, I thought of Integrity. So, I wasn't surprised when he was invited to speak on the subject at a UNI symposium, which I attended in 1986.

Mr. Davis detailed how, as their Control-O-Fax business had grown rapidly to hundreds of employees, incidents of unethical behavior were beginning to surface. A few of his employees were shading the truth or cutting corners to make, or save, a few bucks for the company.

T. Wayne put a stop to this shortsighted practice by instituting training sessions for all his managers on the *Rotary Club's Four Way Test:*

1. *Is it the truth?*
2. *Is it fair to all concerned?*
3. *Will it build goodwill and better friendship?*
4. *Will it be beneficial to all concerned*

I was impressed that integrity could be codified and cultivated to some degree. The little voice in your head will usually tell you what's right or wrong, however this Rotary test is handy if you want your business to be around for a long time. Word gets around fast.

THE MATT PARROTT & SONS COMPANY was founded in 1868, eight years before Gen. Custer's Last Stand at the Little Big Horn. This office products and printing firm hired us as their agency in 1986.

Mr. David Buck is the CEO and majority stockholder of Matt Parrott. In 1991, he approved my idea to hold a Showcase-type event in our local convention center.

We included lots of his vendor's booths and several seminars for customers on office products/systems and printing. It turned out to be a huge success. It continues to this day as a Chamber of Commerce sponsored springtime event: the Grand Slam.

Mr. Buck is a long-time Rotary member and national office holder in that service club. Dave agreed to include a seminar on Integrity if I could entice now-retired Mr. Davis to be the speaker. T. Wayne accepted my invitation. His presentation was well attended and lent prestige to the entire agenda.

That day turned out to be the last time Beverly and I were up close and personal with my beloved friend and mentor. In 1992, T. Wayne Davis died at age

71 in West Palm Beach, Florida. For thirty-one years he'd never disappointed me. Once, he co-signed a short-term down payment note for our first home. All these years after his death, I still miss him. We had some great times together.

The idea for some sort of memorial Integrity Award began to ripen in my mind. How to swing it?

One day in 1994 I shared my Award thoughts with Mr. Dave Buck during one of our marketing meetings. I explained how Davis had epitomized Integrity for me, and inspired me to operate our modest business within Absolutely Straight-Arrow boundaries.

"How about the Matt Parrott Company sponsoring something like that?" Dave asked.

"Let me think about that," I said.

Wise, white-bearded Matt Parrott himself (1837–1900) was quite a pillar of the community: School board, Mayor of Waterloo—re-elected by vote of 1,041 to 9—Iowa State Senator, Official Book Binder, Lt. Governor, President of the National Press Association.

In order for an Award to have longevity, it first must have credibility to make it worthwhile. The Matt Parrott Company does have a sterling reputation: they print over 50-percent of all the voting ballots in the state of Iowa; their relationship with businesses and institutions goes back over 130 years in many cases.

One parallel comes to mind: The Maytag Repairman image works so well, because the Maytag products *really are* so dependable. It's not just hype and hot air PR.

And so, in 1995 we introduced the Matt Parrott Integrity Awards. For three individuals within: 1) Agribusiness, 2) Business & Professional, 3) Education, Government, Not-for-profit. (Full Disclosure: These are the three main categories of Matt Parrott customers and potential business).

Judging is by professionals from the Agribusiness Assoc. of Iowa, Iowa Public Television, and the University of Northern Iowa. Winners are announced at the annual Business Celebration Week Breakfast at UNI. Each recipient also gets a $500 cash prize.

Here's some of the Award nomination copy:

"The Award recognizes the relationship between integrity and leadership. Leadership is the art and technique of influencing individuals or groups to work together with enthusiasm, dedication and skill, toward a common goal.

"Integrity is a vital characteristic of leadership. One must adhere to a code of ethics and moral values without compromise. One must carefully avoid deviousness; utter sincerity, honesty and candor are requisites of strong leadership."

So far, we've honored over thirty outstanding individuals from all walks of life. Our client, Dave Buck, continues his generous support with the firm conviction that this long-term PR campaign reflects well on his company. Comments from the creme de la creme Breakfast audience agree.

(Full details: see mattparrott.com/integrity.html)

Be honest. You'll be happier in your work, get more referrals and recommendations. It really does pay.

27. The World Wide Web; Weblogs (BLOGS)

BETWEEN THE GLEAM in Johann Gutenberg's eye when he invented moveable type in 1452, and the click of Tim Berners-Lee's mouse as he invented the World Wide Web in 1989, lies the first major revolution in the development of communications.

Gutenberg's printing of a cheap Bible put the power of information and religious leadership into the hands of the masses. He became the most *influential* person of the millennium: Ahead of Shakespeare, Martin Luther, Charles Darwin, and Isaac Newton. Without printing, they were destined to be nonentities in history.

Even Christopher Columbus's maps were *printed.*

According to eighty-nine year old Peter Drucker's book, *Management's Challenges in the 21st Century,* Gutenberg's invention made wealthy, powerful men out of technician printers. Their preeminence wasn't surpassed for a hundred years, until the German publishers—like Bertelsmann—gained power through the delivery of *C-O-N-T-E-N-T.*

Then, the printers became craftsmen and the publishers became the princes.

In 1989, the second major revolution in the development of communications began in Geneva, where a young Oxford graduate worked at the CERN Particle Accelerator project. He wanted to connect all their computers via the Internet somehow.

Englishman Tim Berners-Lee made a proposal to his management, which included his original ideas for a "World Wide Web": HTTP hypertext, HTML pages, and URL addresses for servers.

Instant success? No way. It took him two years to get the CERN phonebook on the WWW.

In September 1991 Mr. Berners-Lee gave a demonstration at the Hypertext Conference in San Antonio. The Buzz began.

Inch by inch the bobsled moved down the icy chute:

The Mosaic browser coming out of the U. of Illinois, Wall Street's Netscape darlings Jim Clark and Marc Andreassen starting the IPO's skyrocketing, America Online's (AOL) march toward 30-million subscribers, Microsoft U-turning on the Internet to become WeStink.com in a Federal courtroom; all adding up to the biggest stock market bubble since Holland's 17th century Tulip Mania. *(i.e. $3 trillion just evaporated).*

Hold on tight, this bobsled is still picking up speed.

Mr. Berners-Lee never cashed in big-time on his own invention, by his own choice. He preferred to remain in the background as Chair of the World Wide Web Consortium at MIT. Setting standards is his thing. He said "The Internet has gone from a passion for computers to a passion for money."

In my opinion, Berners-Lee is to Computers what Gutenberg was to the Press. He alone created this second major communications revolution: ALL the people can have ALL the information ALL the time.

[It's now Sir Tim: He was awarded a knighthood in 2004].

Enough history. Now, how did all this high-tech revolution affect our low-tech small business?

COMPUTERS WERE NOT MY THING. In 1995 I still agreed with Mel Grayson, who wrote in *Home Office Computing* magazine, "that computers were like rabies shots: If you have rabies, they can save your life; if you don't, all they do is waste time and money and cause pain. They're counter-productive mischief-makers if you don't need one. And I don't."

And I didn't either.

Everybody around me used computers: Danilo did all our artwork on his Mac; our clients all had the latest whiz-bangs for word processing, inventory control and spread sheets, but I did just fine with my #2 yellow Dixon TICONDERO-GA pencils.

I pencilled my advertising copy and Beverly typed it on her state of the art IBM Quietwriter. Almost all of our copywriting projects are fairly short; it's not like writing a book or feature article.

I'd been tracking the growth of the World Wide Web from the beginning in the Wall Street Journal and other trade publications. Our clients were starting to ask questions throughout 1995.

I vividly recall a full page *WSJournal* WWW feature, wherein the reporter's assignment was to purchase and pay for a book, a music CD and a pair of jeans on the Web. Starting at 8 AM, she recorded all her clicks/steps and sites she visited, her coffee breaks, her lunch and frustrations. By late afternoon, she'd bought the book and CD but gave up on the jeans.

Then, she hopped into her car, drove to the mall, bought all three items on her credit card and was back home, all in forty-five minutes.

B-I-N-G-O! The scales fell from my eyes. You can buy ordinary items at the mall easier than on the Web.

But you cannot buy a Lattner steam boiler at the mall. You have to go searching for seldom-purchased industrial Business-to-Business products. The Web was going to be perfect for our clients.

Eventually then, in January of 1996, I spent several afternoons on the free Internet computer—by appointment—at the Cedar Falls Public Library. On the 18th I barely got home through a blizzard of 8-inches of snow with 40-MPH winds. I was doing our early research to design our very first website, for Lattner Boiler. (lattner.com)

Mr. Steve Junge gave us the approval to write, design and supervise the technical set-up phase. By the time the hosting service provider completed the set-up, our Waterloo Library had established their very first computer for free browsing on the Web. [In late 2003, the Library averaged 250 Web users per day on 16 computers].

That's where I proofread Lattner's pages before it was opened to the world. It was a *so cool* to see my work come up on screen for the first time. [By 2004, Lattner was averaging 3,000 visitors per month for mere pennies per visit].

While other agency executives were attending seminars about the Internet, I was doing the hands-on creative work. It's a collaborative process, but like all of our work, it starts with the writer's concepts.

After Lattner we created websites for the Iowa-Nebraska Farm Equipment Dealers Assoc., and the Iowa Assoc. of Co-Ops. This new source of steady income for the agency has continued: See henkelconstruction.com (forty pages).

When Danilo completed our creative work on the new website for our Matt Parrott & Sons account, I went shopping for quotations to do the technical set-up and hosting service. What I found were two of the nicest people I've ever worked with as suppliers and clients.

Danilo referred me to one of his studio clients who was doing hosting and technical support for the Web: PageTek is a division of Collision Services, Inc.

COLLISION SERVICES, INC

BOB AND CINDY RICHARDS operate several enterprises, all related to the collision repair industry. Their 14,000 customers are bodyshop owners and multi-location executives in this vertical market of 65,000 bodyshops in the USA. CSI provides business forms and stationery, equipment, plus promotional and marketing tools.

Mr. Richards grew up in nearby Hudson, Iowa. He started his own bodyshop in his parent's garage. He moved, then expanded; he hired and trained technicians, finally he founded CSI to serve his chosen industry in 1986.

This entrepreneur's entrepreneur got into printing, computers and software, catalog marketing, website design and hosting, plus developed a valuable national reputation with his Productivity & Marketing Seminars for bodyshop owners. Does he ever sleep?

Mr. Richards was honored as one of the "Top 25 Industry Leaders of the 20th Century" by *Automotive Body Repair News*.

PageTek/CSI had the winning estimate for the Matt Parrott set-up and hosting. When we had our first meeting in his nondescript metal buildings, tucked away in Hudson with fifty employees working like rabbits in a warren, it was Mr. David Stanley finding Dr. Livingston in Africa again:

"I presume you do website hosting *here*?" I said.

"Yes … And by the way, do you happen to know anything about direct mail advertising?" Bob asked.

"Some," I said. That was over eight years and many direct mail packages ago, plus brochures, ads, posters, and website projects working with many of his staff.

CSI is still one of our full-service clients. We help them with advertising and marketing; they help us with websites and printing. Symbiosis is grand.

MS. CINDY RICHARDS is the editor and webmeister for CSI's websites. When we first started working together, CSI was maintaining two websites: one for consumers seeking bodyshop resources, and a second for the bodyshop owners/collision repair industry.

In spite of a black screen with reverse white type—a real pain for your sore eyeballs—Cindy's AutobodyOnline.com (ABOL) had about 1,000 visitors per week. It may have been a bit crude at that point, however she was way ahead of anybody else.

After studying their business, we looked at Meredith's Successful Farming/agriculture.com as a model for an industry/trade hubsite. It's *the* website for farmers and all of agribusiness.

Then, we combined Cindy's two sites into one by *segmenting the visitors when they arrived at the opening screen*. We got rid of the black screen pronto, and added Collision Service's name above the logo for ABOL, so every visitor gets a reminder of the publisher's stake in the industry: The Halo Effect of good PR plus the links to the CSI web catalog.

Ms. Cindy Richards feeds this beast of a black hole with editorial, provides the chatrooms and discussion pages for everybody in their industry, plus sends a weekly newsletter by permission only.

There is a constant natural conflict between the bodyshops and the auto insurance industry, which provides plenty of fat in the fire every day for the discussion pages.

As of this writing, AutobodyOnline.com has 27,000 visitors per week. Check it out to see how Cindy does it. ABOL is tops on all the search engines. *[Grow where you're planted, whether it's Hudson, Hannibal or Halifax].*

ADVANCED HEAT TREAT CORP.

ANOTHER GOOD EXAMPLE of our continuing website creative work, is ahtweb.com for our client Advanced Heat Treat Corp here in Waterloo. In 1989, when Tim Berners-Lee was inventing his WWW, Mr. Gary Sharp was interviewing ad agencies to handle his industrial account. He picked our agency.

Over the years, we created a brand name for all of AHT's heat treating services: UltraGlow for UltraWear, which extends wear 200–800% on steel and cast iron parts for customers like Ford, John Deere and hundreds of other famous companies. We created top-shelf folders and brochures to present the image of one of the most successful heat-treat companies in the world.

Mr. Sharp's company has expanded constantly with three service centers in two states. He's recruited and motivated about 100 employees: Expert technicians and support staff like Marketing Coordinator, Ms. Janet Kern. She helps keep our agency on task. Ms. Janet is another prime example of the energy, honesty and enthusiasm required for successful customer contact positions.

When Gary's not traveling the USA for business, he's enjoying his passion of sailing on Lake Pipin in the upper Mississippi River. He learned integrity and leadership go together early in life, as an outstanding quarterback for his East High school football team.

If you go to the Google.com search engine—my favorite—and enter "ion nitriding," a sophisticated heat treat process, ahtweb.com will come up near the top every time. That's because we've included the behind-the-screen factors, which affect all search engines.

"Meta Tags" are installed on all our client's websites, consistent with search engine good-practices guidelines: not to exceed the number of words in each category.

Try this: Go to ahtweb.com, then click on your View link, when the menu drops down click on Source.

Next you'll see a Notepad image with all the "Meta Tag" words for this website: Title, Description and Keywords. (Of course, you can do these steps for *any* website to view this behind-the screen data). These are the words that separate the men from the boys; take your time and get it right.

You'll notice on the ahtweb.com homepage how we segment the services a specifying engineer may be looking for. Yet, I believe we are able to keep a clean and simple look, which is always our goal for all of our creative. *"More words count less."—Toa Te Ching*

My friend, Dr. Steve Corbin, gave me a copy of *Permission Marketing* by Seth Godin, which details a philosophy of getting a prospect's permission to send more targeted information. The goal isn't just to have a high visitor count, but to be able to establish a relationship with regular visitors. Makes sense when you think about it.

Author Godin says, "Permission Marketing turns strangers into friends, then turns friends into customers."

We're able to track all the data on visitors to the nth degree. The data is confidential, however our clients are extremely pleased with their investments on the WWW. I believe it's terribly cheap compared to other forms of business-to-business media.

Weblogs or BLOGS

As the 21st Century began the popularity of weblogs soared. Known as blogs—an ugly word—they are fantastically easy to set up and super cheap. You need not know anything about HTML programming. All entries are made in normal keyboard English on a simple editing page interface.

Essentially, you have one endless page on the Web with dated entries in the form of a journal or diary. You can add images in a snap to combine words with pictures for reader interest. Others can post to your blog from anywhere in the world; it's ideal for collaboration on projects or multiply authors.

Suddenly, in the fall of 2002, I was an internationally published author on the Web. For about $100 in software costs, I established our weblog to gain hands-on experience and offer timely items for the amusement of our friends and family.

I got lucky by picking a software package called Blogger.com, which was later acquired by Google, meaning only good things to come in the way of innovation and improved customer support.

At this writing our address is http://robertmccusker.blogs.com/mccusker commentary. This medium is exploding exponentially, so I will avoid getting into detail, which would be quickly dated.

Aside from being potential moneymakers, blogs are electronic musings of those self-important nobodies who can't bear to keep their thoughts to themselves—guys like me.

By 2004, some popular 'bloggerpreneurs' discovered their readers would tolerate advertising to keep their pet interest-info coming. Some blogs were bringing in $4–5 thousand per month for their authors. *Way Cool … Blog On!*

The debate over sales taxes for the Internet continues.

My favorite anecdote: The Mayor of Dallas said that if the local Internet companies "didn't start paying their fair share of taxes, the next time one of them called in a fire alarm, he'd fax them a picture of a firetruck." HAR!

SUMMING UP:

Was I correct back in 1995 about the Web being great for our business-to-business clients? According to the *Wall Street Journal:* In 2002, B-2-B Web sales were $482 billion compared to $71 billion to consumers.

While the World Wide Web has morphed into a mainstream means to an end, it remains a rare hybrid: It's a bit like television, direct mail, daily diary, outdoor billboards, classified, newspapers and magazines, newsletters and even early radio. It's all of these things … Rolled into the biggest communications revolution in 550 years. Lucky you. Thanks to Tim Berners-Lee.

VII: SHARING YOUR SUCCESS

"As she walked across the street toward us, I could see how that scrawny, little Beverly Ann Wood had rounded out nicely to a five-foot-two, perfectly-proportioned petite hundred pounder. A Looker! A Keeper! Off the porch I bounded, hormones raging."

Beverly Ann Wood, and Robert, the day before their wedding in 1956.

Mr. Paul Hawken wrote in "*Growing a Business*" in 1988, "It's great if you can have a partner from day one, to share all the trials and triumphs."

Twelve years later: Robert, with children clockwise: Pat, Tom, Dave, Mark and Annie in Chattanooga, TN. McCusker's first attempt at entrepreneurship would fail a few years later after returning to his roots in the Midwest. He later realized that was a real blessing: It prevented him spending a lifetime in a business he actually hated.

28. My Partner, Lady Beverly

THE FIRST TIME I EVER LAID EYES ON HER, she was outdoors building a snowman with Rosie Davidson, back in the old neighborhood. She and Rosie were about thirteen, but Rosie had a big lead on her in the development department.

My pal, Bobby Goings, said "Let's duck'em in a snow bank ... I'll take Rosie." *Who wouldn't?*

So, that's how we met. I pushed Beverly into the nearest snow bank and sat on her. *Meanie!*

She was scrawny but cute, and feisty, I was lucky that terrier-like little lady didn't bite me.

Beverly Ann Wood was new in the neighborhood. She had boundless vitality for whatever she was doing, and she's always doing something.

She was the daughter of Irene and a John Deere tractor works metalwork craftsman. "Woodie" worked in the product development center, where he fashioned prototype parts for design engineers. Mr. Wood treated me with respect all of his life. (Little did he know, Bobby and I tipped over his outhouse one Halloween. HAR!)

As we went through high school, I dated some of the other girls in Beverly's potluck club. We never really warmed up to each other, as she turned into a proper young lady. But she was friendly and vivacious, when we all piled into Eddie Brown's black Buick hearse for a cruise on the strip, then MexiBurgers and root beer at the SnoCap drive-in. *It was 1952 American Graffiti in a fly-over prairie state.*

Beverly was an excellent student and involved with many activities at East High school. That's where she began her lifelong career of live acting on stage.

Beverly is six months older—ssshhhh—than I, and she was one year ahead in school. She graduated high school in 1953, then went to work as a secretary at Rath Packing Company; a nice pink-collar job with a then-prosperous employer of 6,000 folks. We hadn't bumped into each other in a while.

Then one day, I was sitting on the porch swing with old George MacFarland, waiting for the bus to take me to my after-school job at the bakery. The bus stopped across the street on it's way to turnaround at the end of the line, before coming back our way again.

When the bus pulled away to reveal the passenger who'd exited, there was a gorgeous young lady in a gray tailored suit, topped with a tastefully selected white pill-box straw hat.

As she walked across the street toward us I could see how that scrawny, little Beverly Ann Wood had rounded out nicely to 5'2"; a perfectly-proportioned petite hundred pounder: *A Keeper! A Looker!*

Off the porch I bounded, hormones raging. I knew I wanted to spend time with Beverly so I asked her for a date.

"How about going to see a live stage play that's coming into town this week?" she replied. "You bet," I said. For our first date, we went to see a professional touring company perform *Mr. Roberts,* a delightful World War II comedy. (Chauffeured by Brother Bill).

We dated all through my senior year of high school. I joined the Marine Corps Reserve as soon as I turned eighteen that November. Soon after I graduated from Sacred Heart High School in 1954, Beverly kissed me goodbye for boot camp at the train depot where I'd sold the Courier as a lad.

Around Thanksgiving I had a furlough in Waterloo on my way to combat training in California. Beverly was the woman I wanted to marry, so we were engaged before I left again. Two years later, within weeks of my discharge we were married in St. John's Church.

Almost fifty years now ... a good start.

Incredibly, Beverly is the same size now as when we were dating. We're like Jack Spratt and his wife: I can eat no fat and she can eat no lean. I'm about up to market weight these days, but only because Beverly is such a fabulous cook as well a superb homemaker.

I'll skip over some of the things she collects: I don't know what readers would think about a person who has over eighty antique cream pitchers and a cabinet full of stuffed "Beanie Babies".

She has hundreds of houseplants, as well as her flower gardens outside. She reads about fifty books every year (fiction), in addition to all the play scripts she reads for the Waterloo Community Playhouse, her second home, *and still has time for four bridge clubs.*

Beverly has acted onstage in productions over the past thirty years. Many times as a lead character such as in *"Steel Magnolias"* and recently, *"On Golden Pond."* She's done every possible stage-crew job, and has always served on the board of directors; twice elected president. *It's in her blood.*

Whenever Beverly gets involved with any organization, fairly soon she's elected into a leadership role: Like her PEO Club—*(Phone Each Other)*. Others must see the integrity and leadership skill that I do. In 2001 she was nominated for the Mayors' Volunteer of the Year Award.

Beverly loves all her children, grandchildren and now great-grandchildren. She shops year around for gifts and cards. We only wish they all lived closer.

Beverly is always light-hearted and playful. She's the most successful person I know, not because she makes lots of money, or because she's well known, but *because she's a happy person.*

In 1998, when we were selling the big old duplex to move into our current story-and-one-half, I had a wake-up call from Father Time. I had a "*minor*" heart attack, but for those few minutes before the ambulance crew arrived, we were trying to find the words to say goodbye. *Scary ... but I had no regrets.*

After a week in the hospital with all sorts of tests, the doctors performed angioplasty and inserted two scaffold-like stents into the one-and-only artery, which was blocked. Beverly was there with her courage.

Apparently, I lived to tell this tale. Everything has gone smoothly since and I feel great. All my years of jogging and walking the links—over 1,000 miles per year—must have paid off. My cholesterol is excellent. I've learned how to remember the good from the bad: HDL is for "Healthy" and LDL is for "Lethal."

All through my heart escapade Beverly handled the agency business, plus kept the house sale moving. She showed how capable she is of making the right decisions. You couldn't find a better business partner.

She is the wisest, most honest and loving person I've ever known. I'm thankful every day that she's here to sustain and support me. She's made my life a piece of cake. I love you Lady Bev.

I'm the lucky boy who opted to wait for the bus that fateful day in 1953. If I'd biked to work that day, I might be dead now from whiskey and wild women.

29. Send New Year's Cards

HOLIDAY GREETING CARDS are a minor item in the grand scheme of marketing your business. However, we recognized a rich opportunity to distinguish ourselves from the thundering herd of Christmas blather messages.

I write a special verse—usually on national affairs—and Danilo has an opportunity to illustrate without my meddling. Our Limited Edition cards arrive during the first week of the new business year. The feedback has been wonderful for the ten years we've done it.

Here are the verses for 2000 and 2002:

Requiem for Our Century

Goodbye, goodbye old friend,
who thought you'd ever end;
you've got a lot to answer for;
why the slaughter! endless war?

In what way can peace be found?
Is there food to go around?
How do we find the next FDR?
And where is my flying car?

What ever became of contempt
for perjury? Are Presidents exempt?
When do we get better schools?
Wider airline seats? Fewer fools?

How do women live longer?
On less pay? Of all your wonder
drugs, is there a pill for youth?
Was Darwin right? What's the truth?

Will high-tech tools add stress
to victims of our own success;
or yield time for those we embrace,
by slowing our own life's pace?

Goodbye, goodbye old friend,
who thought you'd ever end?

1 January 2000

Dusty Heroes in Twisted Steel

Zealots shriek, "Allah is Great"
as highjacked Innocents pray;
Fanatics crash thousands of lives
and Liberty cries in the bay.

America was inspired
by dusty heroes in twisted steel,
and brave passenger Beamer's
battlecry, as he urged "Let's roll."

1 January 2002

VIII: SUMMARY & REVIEW

"You're the example. You set the tone. You are responsible for the morale of the troops. As the Marine Corps has proven for 225 plus years: You cannot manage men to die for their country, you must lead them into battle."

Esprit de Corps:
The Four E's in Entrepreneur

U.S. Marines landing at Inchon, South Korea, on 15 September 1950. The attack was so swift that casualties were surprisingly low.

30. The Four E's in Entrepreneur

DO YOU REALLY have to be intensely independent and fanatically focused to be a success as a self-employed entrepreneur? Do you need a ton of money to get started with your enterprise? Can you handle the emotional ups and downs—the floods and droughts—of growing your own garden of commerce?

We've covered a lot of ground since the first page in this little book. I've attempted to avoid hard and fast rules. Nevertheless, here are some personal characteristics worthy of mention ... some clues to what works in the real world.

Esprit de Corps: Your energetic, enthusiastic, eager-beaver attitude is contagious to others around you; customers, employees, bankers and prospects are watching you like a hawk all the time.

You're the example. You set the tone. You are responsible for the morale of the troops. As the Marine Corps has proven for 225 plus years: You cannot manage men to die for their country, you must lead them into battle.

Experience: Make certain you know the business you're getting into. Keep your mistakes small. Be patient, keep working for someone else for as long as required to develop the skills and judgement to make profitable decisions. Feed your mind, feed your mind, feed your mind.

"Thus, a great tailor cuts little.
If you try to cut wood like a master carpenter,
you will only hurt your hand."
~ Loa Tsu, 600 BCE

Economical: "Too much money corrupts, because people use it to plug leaks, rather than fix the problems," said Sky Dayton, founder of Earthlink Internet services. Fix the details and the big things will take care of themselves.

If you don't focus on saving money on the little things, you'll be unable to be generous with your employee benefits ... Learn to throw quarters around like manhole covers. Again, if you set the example of economy, others are watching to pick up your habits.

Ethical: If you combine honestly with horse sense, you will have achieved what is most important in business: The ability to deal with people. Then, your good reputation will precede you.

All of our long-term clients have been around for decades and some for over a century. Their ethics have earned them a precious reputation for integrity and leadership in their respective fields. They knew that "Sweet flowers are slow, and weeds make haste," so they prevent weed growth in their business dealings.

THERE ARE MANY MORE words beginning with the letter E that apply to being a successful entrepreneur: Endurance, employer, excellence, effective, endeavor, education … far too many to remember.

If you keep handy the four above, in bold type, I'd judge your chances greatly improved over the next lady or gentleman.

31. Ten Success Secrets You Need to Remember

SUMMING UP: I believe in sound fundamentals and methods. *Methodos* is Greek for "a going after, a way." Here are the BREAK FREE WAY key fundmentals:

1) Identify Your Customers: This is the mother principle of entrepreneurship. Without customers you cannot grow your business. You must know who they are, or where they'll come from: survey to learn how long it will take to get them creating your cash flow.

2) You become what you think about: Take time out to think. We cannot escape our destiny. So be careful what you're thinking about: "Thoughts become words, words become deeds, deeds become habits, and our habits become our destiny."—*Unknown*

3) Concentration X Repetition = Effectiveness. These are the twin battering rams for new business. Specialize, focus on your target market. Remember, Babe Ruth struck out 1,330 times. Talent becomes *valuable* only with your added determination.

4) Invest in yourself. Your education should never end until you're planted in the marble orchard. You're responsible for your physical and mental health. Get out and meet new people. Feed your mind, feed your mind, feed your mind.

5) Get Paid. Concise written understandings in your file drawer are worth more than all the hot air promises of potential in the world. "In reality, people do not want to give you their money—*you have to negotiate it from them.*"—*Robert Ringer*

6) AIDA. Attention, Interest, Desire and Action. This is a model for presenting your ideas, arguments, sales messages or any form of communications. It's been around so long it's generic … the author is Unknown. However, it never fails.

7) Think long-term. Short-term patching of problems will keep you so busy you'll be unable to grow your business and move ahead. Face your difficulties, then you won't have to experience them again and again; remember the Crazy Horse memorial.

8) Do what you do best and hire the rest. This theory of Comparative Value tells you it's wiser to hire others to do some tasks rather than trying to burn the candle at both ends. You may think you're Superman or Wonder Women, but you ain't; you're human.

9) Integrity and Leadership. Be honest. You'll be happier in your work and get more referrals and recommendations. If you want your business to be around for a long time, then you must deal honestly and fairly with everyone you come into contact with.

10) The simple life sets you free. BREAK FREE from the tethers of technology. Loose the bindings of your cell-phone-pager cocoon. "Will high-tech tools add stress/to victims of our own success;/or yield time for those we embrace,/by slowing our own life's pace?"—*RFM, 2000*

EPILOGUE ...

'The Rag on the Bush'

SHE WAS PANTING SOME when she jogged up to me as I walked toward the thirteenth green at Byrnes Park. It was the 12th of April, the day after Beverly's birthday. After an all day spring rain the temperature fell and the wind was howling at 30-MPH, the wind chill was about 20-degrees: A five-layer day.

I was a bit curious to see this slightly stout teenager playing golf by herself; at that age they seldom go to the Girls room by themselves. Must be an emergency.

"Sir, what is the penalty for hitting your ball into a water hazard?" she puffed.

I could see her bag laying in the fourth fairway, just in front of the run-off ditch filled with last night's deluge.

"Well, there's no penalty for hitting into that ditch. That's what's called 'Casual water' in the rulebook," I said. "Just drop your ball back one club length, no closer to the hole and play on."

"Oh no, I'm not asking for me," she said.

"My girlfriend was late, so I started out by myself. Now she just called me on my cellphone ... she's back on number three ... she hit her ball into the pond on the right side ... needs to know what the penalty is?"

"She called you on a cellphone about a ruling?" I asked.

"Yes, just as I was getting ready to swing," she said.

"You tell her that pond is a lateral water hazard: She drops two club lengths from where her ball went into the hazard ... penalty, one stroke," I said. "Then tell her the next time she needs a ruling to call the Pro Shop ... and you turn off your phone to enjoy this time away from civilization."

"Thanks" she grinned, "I'll turn it off right now."

As she jogged back over to her golf bag, my mother's old country saying came to mind:

"Well if that ain't the rag on the bush," Mom would say.

When Mom was a farm girl, before electricity and clothes dryers, her chore was to hang the laundry on the line. Usually there were more clothes than there was clothesline. Nothing was ever thrown away, so there were always rags at the bottom of the wash basket. When the clothesline was full, the rags were hung on the bushes nearby.

When you got to the rags, you were at the end of the line. So, in the country in those days, saying "The rag on the bush," meant "Ain't that the livin' end!"

For me, the girls on the golf course, in weather like that, playing by themselves, *talking on the telephone:*

Well if that ain't the rag on the bush!

When will we ever learn: *It's the simple life that sets us free.*

THIS LAST STORY is the rag on the bush for this tale. I'm at the end of my line. I've hung it all out.

Our journey of a thousand miles leads us right back to our beginning. So, I'll wish you luck and end my yarn with the same sentence it began with:

If you want to grow your own business, you can.

Finally, I'll stop with the same wee word it started with:

If.

~ Robert F. McCusker
January 2005

ACKNOWLEDGEMENTS

Two writers who gave unstintingly of their time and talent from the very first were Steven Maravetz and, my brother, William E. McCusker. Together, they helped shape the structure, then pointed out nail heads to be pounded down: My heartfelt thanks.

When Merrill Oster's generous Foreward scrolled up on my screen, I realized how our clients must feel when they get an important product endorsement for a new product: It feels great.

For their generous support in a variety of ways, I'm grateful to Mark Niedert, Judy Fox Wood, John Cessna, Chuck Gardner, John Doak, Tim McCusker, Tom, Dave, Annie, Mark, and Pat McCusker, Bob and Cindy Richards, Cori Moriarty, Steve Junge, Gary Sharp, Janet Kern, Pat Kinney, Dave Buck, Craig Wohlers, Daryl Grieman, Tom Schaefer, Mark Baldwin, Bill Greer, Trevor Holman, James A. Autry, Jan Kilgard, Lindy McGrane, Monte Meyer, Wylie Burns, Matt Wagner, Andy Devine, Richard Rhodes, Michael Snell, Brian Tarcy, Mike Klassen.

I was lucky to find five bosses who knew enough to teach me some good things: Larry Bailey, Marv Klepfer, T. Wayne Davis, Duane Swensen and Frank Cooper. *Entrepreneurs like me can be a real pain.*

A special salute to my academic friend, Dr. Steve Corbin of the UNI College of Business ... And Leonard Keefe, who taught us both so long ago.

Lady Beverly and Danilo Damjanovic get their kudos inside this book.

SERVICES AVAILABLE

Robert and Beverly McCusker work with a handful of companies on their communications and marketing programs: Consulting, Projects or Full-Service.

Robert McCusker may be interested in speaking at your meeting or to your organization if it's fair and beneficial to all parties.

To find out more about having the McCuskers work with your organization, or having Robert speak to your group, please contact:

McCusker & McCusker
Advertising & Marketing
2314 West 7th Street
Waterloo, Iowa 50702

319–235–6009
rfmccusker@mchsi.com

ABOUT THE AUTHOR

After graduating with a Bachelor of Arts—not Summa Cum Laude, but Thanka De Lorde—in Business Education from Iowa State Teachers College in 1960, Robert F. McCusker spent twelve successful years in sales and sales management in the Office Products field. Then, his first effort as an independent business forms entrepreneur failed.

His long march searching for enjoyable work was rewarded when he fell into advertising and marketing. He worked with an art studio, a graphics and printing center, and an advertising agency.

In 1985, at age fifty, he successfully launched his own ad agency with his wife, Beverly, as his partner; specializing in Business-to-Business clientele. He's the copywriter and creative, Beverly watches the money.

The partners continue to operate their agency on a semi-retired, flexible-lifestyle basis, with a select group of long-time clients—one for over 25 years.

McCusker is a sorry golfer. He hides out most afternoons on the golf courses in the Cedar Valley of Northeast Iowa.

0-595-34427-5

www.ingramcontent.com/pod-product-compliance
Lightning Source LLC
Chambersburg PA
CBHW030802180526
45163CB00003B/1141